QUICK WIN

HR IRELAND

Answers to your top 100

Irish HR questions

Angela Carr

Published by
OAK TREE PRESS
19 Rutland Street, Cork, Ireland
www.oaktreepress.com

A catalogue record of this book is
available from the British Library.

ISBN 978 1 904887 80 5 (Paperback)
ISBN 978 1 904887 81 2 (ePub)
ISBN 978 1 904887 82 9 (Kindle)

DISCLAIMER

This book provides information that has been carefully researched
and presented. Neither Oak Tree Press nor the author can accept
responsibility for the consequences of reliance placed by the reader
on any information in this book. It is important that any reader takes
case-specific legal advice from their HR or legal advisor when such
advice is required.

INTRODUCTION

QUICK WIN HR IRELAND is aimed at owners and managers of small businesses and others in the workplace who manage staff, as well as HR practitioners.

It provides concise, yet informative, answers to the most frequently asked questions about HR and staff issues in an Irish context. It provides simple and practical guidance that can be readily applied. And, for the old-hand, it provides an ideal opportunity to take stock and consider your talents in the light of best practice HR principles.

Like other titles in the **QUICK WIN** series, **QUICK WIN HR IRELAND** is designed so that you can dip in and out of the content as the need arises to search for answers to your top HR questions. There are five sections:

- HR Basics.
- Before Employment.
- During Employment.
- After Employment.
- HR Management.

HR Basics covers key human resource issues applicable to virtually every organisation.

Before Employment looks at the issues arising in advance of employing staff – primarily, but not limited to recruitment.

During Employment covers a wide range of issues likely to arise during an individual's employment, across policy, procedures, performance management, leave and responsibilities for health and safety and dignity at work.

After Employment focuses on the reality of termination of employment – when and how and the issues that might arise afterwards.

HR Management looks at HR's higher level responsibilities to the organisation it serves.

In addition, using the grid in the **Contents** section, you can search for questions and answers across a range of topics:

- Communication.
- Development.
- Management.
- Pay & Benefits.
- Policy & Procedures.
- Recruitment.
- Termination.

And, where appropriate, answers cross-reference to other questions for a fuller explanation or more information.

Enjoy the book – I wish you lots of quick wins and success in your HR role!

Angela Carr
Drogheda
August 2011

ACKNOWLEDGEMENTS

I would like to take this opportunity to thank my colleague Wendy Doyle, of Wendy Doyle Solicitors, for her expert advice and input.

DEDICATION

For John, PJ and Miss Julia

To Michael and Teresa, my parents

Thank you always.

CONTENTS

Search by theme:

HR Basics	**1**
Before Employment	**17**
During Employment	**79**
After Employment	**151**
HR Management	**175**

Or search by topic:

- Communication
- Development
- Management
- Pay & Benefits
- Policy & Procedures
- Recruitment
- Termination

using the grid overleaf.

Bibliography	**181**
About the Author	**183**
The Quick Win series	**184**

HR BASICS	Communication	Development	Management	Pay & Benefits	Policy & Procedures	Recruitment	Termination	Page
Q1 We want to recruit someone, where do we start?						☑		2
Q2 How do we establish our staffing needs?			☑			☑		5
Q3 How do we decide between doing work in-house and outsourcing it?			☑		☑	☑		7
Q4 What must we consult employees on, and when?	☑		☑					9
Q5 How do we identify what training employees need?		☑		☑				10
Q6 What should be included in an employee handbook?	☑		☑					12
Q7 How do we communicate our employee handbook and its contents to employees?	☑		☑					14

BEFORE EMPLOYMENT	Communication	Development	Management	Pay & Benefits	Policy & Procedures	Recruitment	Termination	Page
Q8 What are the key steps in the recruitment process?						☑		18
Q9 How do we define what responsibilities a new job should have?						☑		20
Q10 What is job evaluation?			☑			☑		21

BEFORE EMPLOYMENT

	Communication	Development	Management	Pay & Benefits	Policy & Procedures	Recruitment	Termination	Page
Q11 What should be included in a remuneration package?				☑		☑		23
Q12 How do we establish a fair remuneration package for a specific job?				☑		☑		25
Q13 When does minimum wage legislation apply?			☑	☑				26
Q14 Is everyone equal when it comes to recruitment?						☑		28
Q15 Can we employ students – and at what age?						☑		30
Q16 What are the best ways to recruit?						☑		32
Q17 How do employee referral schemes work?						☑		34
Q18 What is headhunting?						☑		36
Q19 If we use an external recruitment consultancy, what are the steps?						☑		38
Q20 How do we know we have shortlisted the right candidates?						☑		41
Q21 Interviewing – is there a right way / best practice?	☑					☑		43
Q22 Who should interview candidates?	☑					☑		45
Q23 How do we assess candidates at interview?	☑					☑		46
Q24 How do we plan for an interview?	☑					☑		48

BEFORE EMPLOYMENT	Communication	Development	Management	Pay & Benefits	Policy & Procedures	Recruitment	Termination	Page
Q25 How do we conduct an interview?	☑					☑		50
Q26 Are there techniques, other than interviewing, that would help us to choose the right candidate?						☑		51
Q27 How do we know we have chosen the right person after the interview process?						☑		52
Q28 What records do we need to keep of the interview process?			☑			☑		53
Q29 How do we protect ourselves from claims of bias or discrimination from unsuccessful candidates?			☑		☑			54
Q30 How do we make a job offer?	☑					☑		55
Q31 Should a job offer be subject to a satisfactory reference check?						☑		56
Q32 Should a job offer be subject to a medical examination?						☑		58
Q33 What do we do if we cannot identify suitable candidates in Ireland and want to recruit from outside Ireland?						☑		60
Q34 How do we manage a recruitment freeze?			☑		☑	☑		62
Q35 What type of employment contract should we offer?				☑		☑		64

BEFORE EMPLOYMENT	Communication	Development	Management	Pay & Benefits	Policy & Procedures	Recruitment	Termination	Page
Q36 What must we include in an employment contract?				☑				66
Q37 Does an employment contract have to be a written contract to be legally binding?				☑				68
Q38 What is probation –and how does it work?			☑					69
Q39 Do we need an induction programme?	☑	☑	☑					7
Q40 What should we include in an induction programme?	☑	☑	☑					71
Q41 What records do we need to hold on our employees?			☑					73
Q42 What information can we hold on unsuccessful candidates – and for how long?			☑					75

DURING EMPLOYMENT	Communication	Development	Management	Pay & Benefits	Policy & Procedures	Recruitment	Termination	Page
Q43 How many days annual leave are employees entitled to?				☑				78
Q44 What public holidays are employees entitled to?				☑				79
Q45 Are all employees entitled to company days?				☑				81

DURING EMPLOYMENT	Communication	Development	Management	Pay & Benefits	Policy & Procedures	Recruitment	Termination	Page
Q46 How should we respond to an employee who requests time off for jury service?				☑				82
Q47 What are female employees' entitlements to maternity leave?				☑				83
Q48 What are female employees' entitlements on their return to work after maternity leave?				☑				87
Q49 What are male employees' entitlements to paternity leave?				☑				89
Q50 Can both parents take parental leave?				☑				90
Q51 What are employees' entitlements to adoptive leave?				☑				92
Q52 What are employees' entitlements to carers' leave?				☑				94
Q53 Who is entitled to sick pay – and for how long?				☑				96
Q54 What compassionate leave should we allow employees?				☑				98
Q55 How should we address dignity and diversity at work?	☑		☑			☑		99
Q56 How do we meet our obligations as an employer under the Working Time Act?			☑		☑			102

DURING EMPLOYMENT	Communication	Development	Management	Pay & Benefits	Policy & Procedures	Recruitment	Termination	Page
Q57 What responsibilities do we have, as an employer, for health and safety?			☑		☑			104
Q58 What responsibilities do employees have for health and safety?			☑					106
Q59 What should we do to provide a healthy and safe environment for employees?			☑		☑			108
Q60 What is performance appraisal?			☑					109
Q61 When and how should we introduce performance appraisal?			☑					110
Q62 How should we conduct a performance review with an employee?	☑		☑					112
Q63 How do we progress promotions fairly?			☑	☑				114
Q64 How do we deal with underperformance by an employee?			☑					115
Q65 How do we support work-life balance for employees?			☑	☑				116
Q66 What should be included in our grievance and disciplinary policies?			☑		☑			118
Q67 What should be included in our grievance procedure?			☑		☑			120
Q68 What should be included in our disciplinary procedure?			☑		☑		☑	122

DURING EMPLOYMENT	Communication	Development	Management	Pay & Benefits	Policy & Procedures	Recruitment	Termination	Page
Q69 What should be included in our disciplinary appeals procedure?			☑		☑		☑	125
Q70 How should our grievance and disciplinary policies be implemented?	☑		☑					126
Q71 Is using a mediator the best option in grievance or disciplinary cases?			☑					128
Q72 Can we prevent employees from joining a trade union?			☑					130
Q73 Are employees entitled to paid time off during working hours to attend to union duties?			☑	☑				132
Q74 How can interns / work placements help us cope with sudden changes in staffing needs?				☑		☑		133
Q75 How do we respond to a request from an employee to work from home occasionally?			☑	☑				135
Q76 How do we manage employees who work from home regularly?			☑	☑	☑			136
Q77 How should we deal with absenteeism?			☑					138
Q78 How do we conduct an investigation into alleged wrongdoing at work by an employee?			☑		☑		☑	140

DURING EMPLOYMENT	Communication	Development	Management	Pay & Benefits	Policy & Procedures	Recruitment	Termination	Page
Q79 Should we have a data protection policy?	☑		☑		☑			142
Q80 What do we do if an employee claims he / she is being bullied or harassed?	☑		☑	☑			☑	144
Q81 What should be included in an email policy?	☑		☑		☑			146
Q82 What pension rights do employees have?				☑				148

AFTER EMPLOYMENT	Communication	Development	Management	Pay & Benefits	Policy & Procedures	Recruitment	Termination	Page
Q83 On what grounds can we terminate an employee's contract?			☑				☑	152
Q84 When is it legal to terminate without a notice period?			☑				☑	154
Q85 What is constructive dismissal?			☑				☑	155
Q86 Should we conduct exit interviews with all leaving employees?	☑		☑				☑	156
Q87 How should we conduct an exit interview?	☑		☑				☑	158

AFTER EMPLOYMENT

	Communication	Development	Management	Pay & Benefits	Policy & Procedures	Recruitment	Termination	Page
Q88 Should we give references to leaving employees – and what should we say / not say?	☑		☑					159
Q89 When is TUPE relevant?			☑	☑			☑	161
Q90 Can we recover pay from a former employee?				☑				164
Q91 Must all employees serve out their notice period?			☑	☑				166
Q92 When is redundancy applicable?							☑	168
Q93 When does last in, first out apply in selecting employees for redundancies?			☑		☑		☑	169
Q94 What steps do we need to take to make someone redundant fairly?			☑		☑		☑	170
Q95 Do we need a confidentiality policy?	☑		☑		☑			171
Q96 We are restructuring our business – where do we start?	☑		☑	☑	☑		☑	172
Q97 What is the difference between redundancy and voluntary severance?				☑	☑		☑	174

HR MANAGEMENT	Communication	Development	Management	Pay & Benefits	Policy & Procedures	Recruitment	Termination	Page
Q98 What is the responsibility of HR in a downturn?	☑		☑					176
Q99 When do we need to employ an interim HR professional?			☑					178
Q100 How do we steal a march on our competitors with a better recruitment experience for candidates?			☑					180

HR BASICS

Q1   We want to recruit someone, where do we start?

Before you begin any recruitment, consider the role you want to fill: is it new or has someone else previously occupied this role? If the latter, are you content it was the right role for the organisation? If not, reconsider the role.

Then document the *role* in a job description, including:

- Job purpose.
- Accountabilities.
- Some context on the role to give clarity on where it sits in the overall structure and plans for your organisation.
- Knowledge and experience required to perform the role satisfactorily (not just the previous job-holder's qualifications).
- Other aspects to the role, including financial or staff responsibilities.

Next, consider the type of *person* you want to recruit. Use a person specification, which should include personal characteristics – for example, communication skills, interpersonal skills, capable of working on one's own initiative.

Last, consider affordability: avoid pitching the role too high or too low.

The steps in hiring a new staff member then are:

- Decide on the recruitment methods you will use:
  - Internal: Advertising internally, employee referral schemes.
  - External: Newspapers, employment agencies, executive search (for senior staff), personal referrals, or online through company website or other websites.
- Screen and shortlist applications:
  - Screen applications in line with the job and person specifications and any other pre-agreed criteria.

- Ensure fairness and equity in the process and that your organisation can stand over all candidates who are requested to attend the next stage of the process.
- Planning the interview:
  - Decide on the type of interview: face-to-face, telephone, biographical or competency-based.
  - Agree on an interview panel.
  - Ensure the interviewers understand in detail the provisions of the *Employment Equality Law Acts 1998 to 2008*, particularly their responsibility to avoid any discriminatory questions.
  - Prepare in advance of the interview by reviewing job and person specifications.

Following the interview and the selection of a preferred candidate, check:

- References (in line with the *Data Protection Acts 1988 to 2003*).
- The eligibility of the person to work (in Ireland).
- Medical examination (*via* a pre employment medical examination or a questionnaire).

It is usual to offer the role to the preferred candidate while these checks are being carried out – the offer of employment being subject to reference and medical checks.

Once the candidate joins your organisation:

- Issue a letter of offer / contract.
- Prepare a staff file.
- Provide induction training.
- Monitor performance during probation.

See also

Q2   How do we establish our staffing needs?
Q8   What are the key steps in the recruitment process?
Q9   How do we define what responsibilities a new job should have?
Q14   Is everyone equal when it comes to recruitment?
Q15   Can we employ students – and at what age?
Q16   What are the best ways to recruit?

Q21   Interviewing – is there a right way / best practice?

Q26   Are there techniques, other than interviewing, that would help us to choose the right candidate?

Q30   How do we make a job offer?

Q31   Should a job offer be subject to a satisfactory reference check?

Q33   What do we do if we cannot identify suitable candidates in Ireland and want to recruit from outside Ireland?

Q35   What type of employment contract should we offer?

Q36   What must we include in an employment contract?

Q38   What is probation –and how does it work?

Q39   Do we need an induction programme?

Q40   What should we include in an induction programme?

Q62   How should we conduct a performance review with an employee?

Q100 How do we steal a march on our competitors with a better recruitment experience for candidates?

Q2 How do we establish our staffing needs?

To establish staffing requirements, planning for recruitment must be closely aligned to your organisation's business planning process. It is impossible to recruit the right people in the right place at the right time otherwise.

Planning for recruitment (manpower planning) should enable the business plan, by forecasting employee demand in line with the achievement of overall objectives for your organisation.

The key activities involved in establishing staffing needs are:

- Understand in detail the numbers and skill set of your current employees – staff headcount numbers (both those in and out of the organisation on any kind of leave or absence) and the current skill set required to meet business targets at present.

- Calculate the actual average time available to an employee at work in a given timeframe (your budget timelines), allowing for annual and public leave, attendance at training courses, absence, any other leave (for example, maternity leave, jury service, *force majeure*, retirements, voluntary severance or other downtime).

- Use this information to develop a demand forecast for employee numbers to deliver to the strategic and business plans.

- Determine the difference between the demand forecast and the actual staff headcount numbers – this is the basis for your recruitment plan.

- Agree timelines and budgets for recruitment.

- Document priority roles immediately – job specifications that are to be sourced immediately – and then plan for all other recruitment in order of priority.

- Evaluate the roles and benchmarks in your markets.

- Begin recruiting.

When recruiting for large numbers of people at the same time (ramp recruitment), demand plans should be signed off in advance of any recruitment. These plans and ultimate recruitment delivery should be reviewed regularly. For example, in call or contact centres, the planning should be done well in advance, working back from the preferred start date of new hires and allowing for any induction or training that might be required before actual start dates. There also may be an opportunity, particularly with large scale recruitment, to outsource or partially outsource the recruitment.

See also
Q3   How do we decide between doing work in-house and outsourcing it?
Q10   What is job evaluation?
Q34   How do we manage a recruitment freeze?
Q74   How can interns / work placements help us cope with sudden changes in staffing needs?
Q100   How do we steal a march on our competitors with a better recruitment experience for candidates?

Q3   How do we decide between doing work in-house and outsourcing it?

Deciding to outsource work has become an increasing trend over the last number of years. Outsourcing HR in large organisations has focused mainly on HR administrative and specialist services, such as recruitment activities, whereas in smaller companies outsourcing has involved everything from HR management to payroll, where HR professionals provide ongoing but not fulltime support. Much of this support focuses on companies' concerns with complying with employment legislation.

When deciding to outsource HR, the main points to consider are:

- Why are we outsourcing? (benefits)
- What are we outsourcing? (specifically)
- Will there be a fall-out as a result of this outsourcing? And, if so, what?
- Will transfer of undertakings (protection of employment) (TUPE) legislation apply or is this work that is currently not being done in-house?

When you have decided that outsourcing is what you want to do, ensure that:

- There is clarity – in-house and with the outsourced provider – about the work to be outsourced (this requires a detailed specification).
- There is a tender process – many companies offer outsourcing services, make sure you chose the right one for your organisation.
- All employee-related aspects are dealt with:
  - Is the work that is being outsourced currently being done (or almost wholly done) by a person or team in-house? If so, there may be a TUPE situation.
  - Ensure staff do not feel that their roles are being reduced as a result of the outsourcing.

- Where possible, ensure staff are fully aware of the outsourcing decision from an early stage – this will enable the outsourcing process to go smoothly, perhaps you should consider engaging some of the staff to work on the outsourcing project.

- The output of the outsourced provider is reviewed regularly to make sure the service is delivering for your organisation.

See also
Q89   When is TUPE relevant?
Q96   We are restructuring our business – where do we start?

Q4   What must we consult employees on, and when?

Most organisations include their staff by consulting with them regarding the future in order to promote employee engagement and positive working relations. However, sometimes, because of a legal requirement or the sensitive nature of a project for example, they cannot include employees on all aspects of the business.

Nonetheless, there are a number of pieces of legislation that outline the statutory rights of employees where they are to be informed and consulted on issues that affect them, including:

- *Provision of Information and Consultation Act 2006.*
- *Code of Practice on Information and Consultation (SI No 132 of 2008).*
- *Protection of Employment Act 1977 (amended by SI No 370 of 1996).*
- *Worker Participation (State Enterprises) Acts 1977 to 2001.*
- *Transnational Information and Consultation of Employees Act 1996.*
- *European Works Council Directive 2009/38/EC* (published 16 May 2009).

Although the intention and detail of these pieces of legislation vary, in essence organisations should consult with employees – and / or their representatives – on anything that may affect them directly or indirectly.

See also
Q89   When is TUPE relevant?
Q96   We are restructuring our business – where do we start?

Q5   How do we identify what training employees need?

Identifying the training your employees need should be a two-way process. Best practice includes training and development as an integral part of the overall performance management process.

Ideally, the process for an individual includes a number of stages for the employee and his / her line manager:

- Set and agree objectives.
- Meet regularly one-to-one to review objectives and discuss areas for improvement and any training or development needs.
- Source jointly the training intervention(s).
- Review at one-to-ones whether the training is going well.
- Review and evaluate in practice whether the training is helping with meeting objectives.

When reviewing the overall training needs for an organisation, a training needs analysis (TNA) often is conducted to gather information, based on:

- Job specifications.
- Person specifications.
- Line manager feedback.
- The performance and skills of employees.

The output from the TNA identifies where there are gaps.

At this point, there may be an opportunity to develop a training (learning) and development plan at organisation level, pulling together common gaps and providing learning and development solutions for the organisation as a whole. This approach should support the process for the individual also.

The two processes – organisational and individual – should not be mutually exclusive unless the company is small in size, where there may not be a requirement to have a detailed companywide plan.

See also

Q39 Do we need an induction programme?
Q40 What should we include in an induction programme?
Q60 What is performance appraisal?
Q61 When and how should we introduce performance appraisal?
Q62 How should we conduct a performance review with an employee?

Q6   What should be included in an employee handbook?

To be sure that you are covering all your employees' statutory rights, the following policies should be included in your organisation's staff handbook:

- Time and attendance:
  - Absenteeism.
  - Time-keeping.
- Sick leave:
  - Sick leave.
  - Absence notification and certification procedures.
  - Compassionate leave.
- Statutory leave:
  - Annual leave and public holidays: The process; applying for holidays; public and company holidays.
  - Maternity leave: Purpose and scope; the policy; employee absence due to sickness; breastfeeding arrangements.
  - Parental and *force majeure* leave: Purpose and scope; protection of employment rights; applying for parental leave; remuneration (pay and superannuation); explaining *force majeure* leave.
  - Adoptive leave: Purpose and scope; protection of rights; returning to work; payment during adoptive leave; adoption classes; postponement of leave / hospitalisation of the child; termination of additional adoptive leave.
  - Carer's leave: Purpose and scope; protection of rights; returning to work.
  - Jury service: Obligation.
- Harassment, bullying and victimisation in the workplace.
- Equal opportunities.
- Health and safety.
- Grievance and disciplinary procedures.
- Confidentiality.

- Data protection.

Other areas that may be covered include:

- Dress code and hygiene.
- Exclusivity of employment.
- Communications, email and internet use.

See also

Q7   How do we communicate our employee handbook and its contents to employees?
Q43   How many days annual leave are employees entitled to?
Q44   What public holidays are employees entitled to?
Q46   How should we respond to an employee who requests time off for jury service?
Q47   What are female employees' entitlements to maternity leave?
Q48   What are female employees' entitlements on their return to work after maternity leave?
Q49   What are male employees' entitlements to paternity leave?
Q50   Can both parents take parental leave?
Q51   What are employees' entitlements to adoptive leave?
Q52   What are employees' entitlements to carers' leave?
Q53   Who is entitled to sick pay – and for how long?
Q54   What compassionate leave should we allow employees?
Q63   How do we progress promotions fairly?
Q66   What should be included in our grievance and disciplinary policies?
Q67   What should be included in our grievance procedure?
Q68   What should be included in our disciplinary procedure?
Q69   What should be included in our disciplinary appeals procedure?
Q70   How should our grievance and disciplinary policies be implemented?
Q77   How should we deal with absenteeism?
Q79   Should we have a data protection policy?
Q80   What do we do if an employee claims he / she is being bullied or harassed?
Q81   What should be included in an email policy?
Q95   Do we need a confidentiality policy?

Q7 How do we communicate our employee handbook and its contents to employees?

Points to consider when communicating a staff handbook for the first time include:

- **The rationale for introducing the handbook:** It is not just about compliance, although do stress the importance of the legislative backdrop. Explain to staff that you want to ensure that your organisation is up-to-date on all employee legislation and that there is a repository for all employee information in one place – making it user-friendly and accessible.

- **The support of senior management:** Ensure you have senior management buy-in from the concept to the implementation and that it is not just an HR initiative. Whether you are part of a large or small organisation, if senior management are not part of the communication, your handbook will fail in terms of staff referring to it.

- **The way in which it is communicated:** This is critical, as there are many ways in which to communicate to staff now, from email to apps. By far the most impactful messaging will be face-to-face with your staff. If this is not feasible, consider online chat, blogs, intranet, external website, DVDs, as well as email and hard copy communications. Decide which best suits your organisation, and have management lead it, with HR support.

- **Give staff the opportunity to review the handbook:** Provide an opportunity for Question and Answer sessions or, at the very least, provide FAQs (Frequently Asked Questions) in a staff newsletter or other communication.

When introducing a staff handbook, consider:

- **Consider what must be included:** The statutory inclusions.

- **Consider what is relevant for your business:** You probably won't need to include a detailed organisation chart if there are only five of you in the organisation!

- **Be practical:** Don't include items that you will not be able to support – for example, reference to bonus schemes that are not discretionary.
- **Keep it up-to-date!** A good idea is to keep someone on a retainer who will update the handbook for you as legislation changes.

It is also worth having each employee sign a statement saying that they have read the new handbook and understand the implications of it.

See also
Q6   What should be included in an employee handbook?
Q99   When do we need to employ an interim HR professional?

BEFORE EMPLOYMENT

Q8   What are the key steps in the recruitment process?

Depending on a number of variables, including the role you are recruiting for, the number of people you want to recruit, whether it's an executive search or contingency-based recruitment, there can be any number of steps in a recruitment process.

In broad terms, however, the essential first steps are to define:

- The role (job specification).
- The type of person you are looking for (person specification).

Once you have decided these two, you can move to recruit. Again, in broad terms, the steps here are:

- **Sourcing and attraction:** Attracting talent to your organisation is one of the most important steps in the recruitment process. Many recruitment campaigns or approaches are not specific enough, and often lead to a plethora of CVs and unlikely / unsuitable candidates for your role, creating unnecessary work for those involved in the process. Use a focused sourcing approach: fish in the right candidate pool! Common sourcing approaches include:
  - Putting an advertisement in the paper – this is still a popular option, as organisations see it as an opportunity to market themselves in the process.
  - Engaging a recruitment agency.
  - Employee referral schemes – many organisations look internally to their own staff to refer friends or colleagues.
  - Online job boards.
  - Executive search or head-hunters for more senior roles.
  - Social networking sites.
  - Apps (for smart phones).
- **Selection and assessment:** This area often generates debate because, even with the introduction of many new techniques for selection, most organisations still like to interview, thus leaving an

element of subjectivity in the process. Techniques used to assess candidates include:

- Biographical interviews.
- Competency-based interviews.
- Psychometric tests.
- Assessment centres.

- **Offer and follow up:** The steps here are:
  - Offer or decline candidates in the timelines you communicated at interview – don't delay.
  - Always offer feedback to all candidates.
  - Offer the role to the successful candidate first – if they decline, then you can offer the role to your second choice candidate.
  - Agree the offer verbally with the successful candidate, and follow up promptly with a letter of offer / written statement of terms of employment.

See also

Q1	We want to recruit someone, where do we start?
Q2	How do we establish our staffing needs?
Q9	How do we define what responsibilities a new job should have?
Q16	What are the best ways to recruit?
Q17	How do employee referral schemes work?
Q18	What is headhunting?
Q19	If we use an external recruitment consultancy, what are the steps?
Q21	Interviewing – is there a right way / best practice?
Q26	Are there techniques, other than interviewing, that would help us to choose the right candidate?
Q29	How do we protect ourselves from claims of bias or discrimination from unsuccessful candidates?
Q30	How do we make a job offer?
Q35	What type of employment contract should we offer?
Q36	What must we include in an employment contract?

Q9   How do we define what responsibilities a new job should have?

When starting to think about a new role and the activities and duties it should include, best practice suggests using job analysis to ensure that you have all the details you need to recruit the best talent in the market for that role.

Job analysis brings clarity to the duties and responsibilities of a role by breaking it down into its component parts, such as:

- **Job description or role profile:** This describes what the role is likely to do, the duties it should undertake and the overall responsibilities of the job. A detailed job description should be drawn up and documented in conjunction with the line manager(s). It should include reporting lines, financial scope, and perhaps even an organisation chart to show where the role fits with the rest of the organisation. It should be signed off by the line manager(s) to show that they have signed up to the role.

- **Job specification:** This brings clarity to the specific skills and abilities the successful person needs in order to perform the role satisfactorily.

- **Person specification:** This sets out what the ideal candidate will have by way of education, experience, and personal qualities. A person specification can help interviewers to select the best person for the role, not just someone they 'like'.

See also
Q10   What is job evaluation?

Q10 What is job evaluation?

Job evaluation is the process of evaluating roles, and comparing them for relativity to other roles across an organisation in a consistent manner. After a job analysis has been carried out, job evaluation helps to size jobs or roles in an organisation.

Job evaluations then can be used in a number of different ways, including:

- Pay and reward.
- Talent and succession planning.
- Organisational (re)structuring and career development.

There are many different job evaluation methodologies and approaches.

General considerations when embarking on a job evaluation include:

- Review the role, not the person.
- If the role being evaluated already exists, evaluate it as it is now, not as it might be / should be.
- Have as much detail as possible (a detailed job description is essential).
- Assume the role operates at a satisfactory level of performance.

To carry out a job evaluation process for a business unit in your organisation:

- Ensure there are detailed job descriptions across the organisation signed off by the line manager(s).
- Ensure that business unit level organisation charts have been signed off also.
- Take a sample role from each level within the business unit structure, and evaluate those first (allowing for relativities when other roles are being evaluated – roles above and below) .
- Establish a job evaluation panel from HR and line management to review and evaluate the job descriptions.

- Using a job evaluation methodology,[1] establish the 'size' of the job relative to other roles in the organisation structure.
- Ensure continuous review – don't assume all job evaluations are 'correct' – review previous sizings against new role sizes and validate.

See also
Q9   How do we define what responsibilities a new job should have?
Q11   What should be included in a remuneration package?
Q96   We are restructuring our business – where do we start?

---

[1]   The Hay Group created and owns the most widely-used job evaluation methodology in the world, used in over 8,000 organisations (**www.haygroup.com**).

Q11 What should be included in a remuneration package?

A number of different pay and benefits elements can be included in a remuneration package, such as (but not limited to):

- Basic pay.
- Variable pay, including bonuses, commission, etc.
- Company cars, fully or partially-expensed.
- Pension schemes.
- Private medical insurance – or a discount for staff and their families if the organisation does not pay the full cost.
- Permanent health insurance, in case staff are unable to work for long periods.
- Annual leave – statutory annual leave must be included – offering leave in excess of this is at the organisation's discretion.
- Other leave – paternity leave, bereavement leave, marriage leave, etc.
- Educational and training support.
- Long-term incentive plans.
- Give-as-you-earn scheme for charitable donations.
- Sports club annual subscription.
- Mortgage subsidy.
- Maternity pay.
- Childcare vouchers.
- Employee assistance programme.
- Employee discount programme.
- Cycle to work scheme.

In some cases, benefits in addition to basic pay are subject to income tax under Benefit-in-Kind (BIK) rules. As a result, the benefit may be less attractive and so, where employees have a choice, they should consider the tax consequences of a benefit before deciding whether to opt for it. Some organisations address this by offering a menu of benefits and allowing employees to choose to make their own selection, within laid-down limits. Depending on an individual employee's level within an organisation, the menu of benefits available to them may be greater or lesser.

See also

Q12   How do we establish a fair remuneration package for a specific job?
Q13   When does minimum wage legislation apply?
Q43   How many days annual leave are employees entitled to?
Q44   What public holidays are employees entitled to?
Q46   How should we respond to an employee who requests time off for jury service?
Q47   What are female employees' entitlements to maternity leave?
Q48   What are female employees' entitlements on their return to work after maternity leave?
Q49   What are male employees' entitlements to paternity leave?
Q50   Can both parents take parental leave?
Q51   What are employees' entitlements to adoptive leave?
Q52   What are employees' entitlements to carers' leave?
Q53   Who is entitled to sick pay – and for how long?
Q54   What compassionate leave should we allow employees?
Q65   How do we support work-life balance for employees?
Q82   What pension rights do employees have?

Q12 How do we establish a fair remuneration package for a specific job?

If the roles in your organisation have been evaluated fairly and objectively, this will make it easier to establish a fair remuneration package since the role can be benchmarked in the market against similar sized roles, independent of the person holding the role.

The first things to consider are affordability and, from a pay perspective, where does your company position itself in the market?

Some organisations want to be market leaders when it comes to remuneration; others are happy to pay fairly but not be a market leader, offering instead other (less expensive to the company) benefits as part of a package.

The overall remuneration package for an individual should look beyond the individual and take into account other relativities in the organisation, including:

- Equal pay for equal work
- Affordability for the long-term, not just this one new hire.
- Relativities to other employees in the company who have been with the organisation for a long time.

Where formal remuneration policies exist – usually in larger organisations – they often are documented (in banking, this is now a given).

See also
Q10 What is job evaluation?
Q11 What should be included in a remuneration package?

Q13   When does minimum wage legislation apply?

Organisations and potential new hires normally negotiate their own rates of pay, but under the *National Minimum Wage Act, 2000* everyone is entitled to a minimum wage[2] with some exceptions – for instance, young people under 18 years are only entitled to 70% of the minimum wage.

Prior to 7 July 2011, when the Labour Court made an Employment Regulation Order (ERO) confirming proposals submitted by a Joint Labour Committee (JLC), the ERO was legally binding on both employers and employees in the industry / sector represented by the JLC. However, following a High Court decision, EROs ceased to have statutory effect from that date. New legislation reforming the JLCs and wage-setting mechanisms is expected to be introduced in late 2011.

Despite this, employees' existing contracts of employment still govern their pay and conditions of work. If an employer reduces an employee's rate of pay, this would be a change in their contract of employment which normally requires the employee's consent.

Pay and conditions of employees who commence work after 7 July 2011 are not subject to EROs but, nonetheless, are governed by the minimum wage legislation.

See also
Q11   What should be included in a remuneration package?
Q12   How do we establish a fair remuneration package for a specific job?

   http://www.citizensinformation.ie/en/employment

---

[2]   At the time of going to print, the *Social Welfare and Pensions Bill, 2011* proposed that the national minimum wage in Ireland would be restored to €8.65 per hour.

Q14 Is everyone equal when it comes to recruitment?

Everyone should be equal when it comes to recruitment, and equality is something that both employees and employers should expect when as part of any recruitment process.

The *Equality Acts, 1998-2008* make it illegal to discriminate in many areas, including pay and recruitment, on the following nine grounds:

- Gender.
- Marital status.
- Family status.
- Sexual orientation.
- Religion.
- Age.
- Disability.
- Race.
- Membership of the travelling community.

Although it is illegal to discriminate on gender grounds, it is not discriminatory to choose someone of a particular gender for a post where:

- Their gender constitutes a genuine and determining occupational requirement for the post.
- The objective is legitimate and the requirement is proportionate.

It is also not illegal for an employer to arrange for or to provide treatment that gives a greater benefit to women in connection with maternity or adoption matters.

Importantly, there are also limited exclusions for the Gardaí and Prison Service, in order to deal with violent situations (for example, a height requirement) and to allow for the appropriate gender balance for the purposes of both these services.

Note that employees are covered by equality legislation from the first day of their employment, and so employers need to be very careful and mindful of employees' rights in this regard. We can never be too equal!

See also
Q12   How do we establish a fair remuneration package for a specific job?
Q29   How do we protect ourselves from claims of bias or discrimination from unsuccessful candidates?
Q47   What are female employees' entitlements to maternity leave?
Q48   What are female employees' entitlements on their return to work after maternity leave?

Q15   Can we employ students – and at what age?

Under the *Protection of Young Persons (Employment) Act, 1996*, a young person is defined as a person who is under 16 years of age or the school-leaving age (whichever is higher – the school-leaving age is currently 16) but is less than 18 years old.

If your company is considering hiring a student (someone under 18yrs), you must (as with any employee):

- Issue a written statement of employment.
- Agree pay, at least in line with the National Minimum Wage Act, 2000.
- Make appropriate provision for the young person's health and safety (including a risk assessment) and to prevent bullying and harassment.

In addition, you should:

- Provide induction, since the young person may not have any previous workplace experience.
- Offer study time, if required – but, at the very least, be mindful of their education.
- Consider the work you are offering, to ensure it is age-appropriate and not beyond their level of ability.
- Obtain written consent from the parents or guardian of the young person.

There is a general prohibition on the employment of children (under-16s), except:

- Where the Minister authorises (by licence) individual cases – for example, in the area of the arts, culture or sports, although this employment must not affect schooling.
- Where the Minister authorises the employment of children over 13 years in cultural or artistic arenas.

- Where employers may employ 14/15-year-olds on light work (1) during the school term, as part of approved work experience or an educational programme or (2) outside of school terms, provided the hours do not exceed seven hours in one day or over 35 hours in a week and the child receives a minimum of 21 days break during the summer holidays.

- Where employers employ children over 15 years of age to do light work during the school term, provided the hours are not more than eight hours per week of work or as part of a training or work experience programme approved by the Minister or FÁS, where such work does not exceed eight hours per day or 40 hours per week.

Also, as an employer, you should ensure that:

- You employ a child only during daytime hours.
- A child employee receives a minimum rest period of 14 consecutive hours in a 24-hour period (this rest period may be interrupted but there are guidelines around that also).
- The child employee receives a minimum of two days rest in a seven-day period and that the rest is consecutive where possible and practical (the rest period may be interrupted but there are guidelines around that also).

You must ensure that a child you employ does not work any longer than four hours before she / he receives a rest break of 30 consecutive minutes. There is no entitlement to payment for such a break.

See also
Q1   We want to recruit someone, where do we start?
Q74   How can interns / work placements help us cope with sudden changes in staffing needs?

Q16 What are the best ways to recruit?

In order to decide the best way to recruit for your organisation, first consider whether you want to recruit internally or externally or a combination of both.

Internal recruitment

Internal recruitment focuses on advertising roles within an organisation through:

- Vacancies posted on notice boards.
- Vacancies posted on a company intranet site.
- Employee referral schemes.

Generally, recruiting internally involves defined processes and procedures, often guided by trade union agreements (in larger organisations), to ensure equality of opportunity for all staff.

When recruiting internally, it is important to ensure that staff on protective leave (maternity or parental leave) are offered the option to apply for any new vacancies.

Some internal recruitment teams have Service Level Agreements (SLAs) with the organisation to ensure that they deliver a professional 'external-like' service.

Most internal recruitment teams exhaust the internal market in an organisation before going to the external market – in some cases, they initiate both at the same time.

The internal market is a good recruitment option in a downturn as it is less costly than going to the external market and the candidate should have a greater understanding of the organisation. On the downside, where an appointment is made another vacancy appears, so there may be a necessity to go to the external market anyhow for a different role.

External recruitment

The most common ways of recruiting externally are:

- Recruitment agencies.
- Executive search / head-hunters.
- Executive research consultants.
- Newspapers / media advertisements.
- On-line job boards.
- The organisation's website.

Finally the best way to recruit may be a combination of internal and external recruitment, but no recruitment will be successful if your recruitment partners do not understand both the role on offer and your organisation – that is the key to any successful recruitment.

See also
Q8   What are the key steps in the recruitment process?
Q17   How do employee referral schemes work?
Q18   What is headhunting?
Q19   If we use an external recruitment consultancy, what are the steps?

Q17   How do employee referral schemes work?

One of the best ways to source good staff is to ask existing employees. Internal employee referral programmes can play a major role in attracting talent.

Referred candidates are more likely to be a good fit for the organisation since they are already prepared for what it might be like to work there already. They also are more likely to settle in and stay longer as a result. Staff rarely refer friends or family unless they think they will be successful.

An employee referral scheme works like this:

- The vacancy is posted in the normal way – on the intranet or external website, for example.
- Staff internally review it and refer a friend or colleague for the role.
- The referred candidate is shortlisted along with all other candidates sourced through other channels.
- If the referred candidate is successful after interview(s), an offer is made in the normal way.
- The staff member who referred the successful candidate is entitled to a referral fee – usually, half this fee is paid when the candidate starts and the other half after they complete probation.
- The criteria for referring friends or colleagues may exclude some categories of staff – for example:
  - Senior managers who may have influence over the recruitment process.
  - Someone recruiting for their own department, as recruitment may be part of their regular duties and responsibilities.
  - Some members of HR, as recruitment may be part of their regular duties and responsibilities.
- The criteria for claiming the referral fee may have exclusions – for example:

- Referral of ex-employees.
- Where the referred candidate came through another source first (through a recruitment agency, perhaps).
- Where the referred candidate is working on a temporary basis with the organisation already, either on a temporary or fixed-term contract or employed through a recruitment agency.

See also
Q16 What are the best ways to recruit?

Q18   What is headhunting?

Executive search (more informally known as headhunting) is a professional service offered to organisations to recruit and fill executive positions.

Usually provided externally, executive search professionals see what they do as entirely different from the work of a typical recruitment agency (known as contingency search). A major difference is that an executive search firm is engaged on a retained basis, which means that part payment is made upfront to initiate the process, then another amount is paid towards the middle of the process and the balance on selection. Thus considerable expense may be incurred without achieving successful recruitment – although this is rare.

Contingency firms, on the other hand, receive their entire fee only at the end of the process, when they have recruited a suitable candidate. Also, importantly, executive search firms nearly always work for and represent an organisation and do not place out-of-work individuals – unlike contingency firms.

Executive search works well where there is a requirement for the client not to advertise the role (because of internal sensitivities), or where previous reputational damage to the organisation means there is a requirement to 'sell' the role to allay any fears a prospective candidate might have.

While executive search firms are costly, ways of reducing the cost include:

- Giving one firm exclusive rights to the assignment and paying only when and if they are successful.
- Giving the assignment to a more established contingency search firm with very clear details of what is expected, including timelines.

- Negotiating – although almost firms state that they do not negotiate on fees, in the current economic climate there may be an opportunity to do so.

Some executive search firms are global firms covering a wide range of industry sectors; others are boutiques that cover only a specific sector (for example, finance).

When engaging with an executive search firm, check for fit with your organisation. Does the firm have the necessary experience and networks to attract the right candidate for you? If not, you may end of paying up to two-thirds of the cost without securing that new MD! That said, when successful, executive search works well: your organisation attracts the right candidate, in the most professional way, while testing the market in the process, and internal candidates are not upset by a large-scale recruitment drive that might send the wrong message to candidates and clients alike.

See also
Q16   What are the best ways to recruit?
Q17   How do employee referral schemes work?

Q19   If we use an external recruitment consultancy, what are the steps?

When your organisation has decided to engage a recruitment agency, the next step is to decide which one and why? There are many recruitment agencies in Ireland: deciding on the right one for your organisation can be difficult.

The steps to consider when engaging an agency are:

- Check whether the agency has a licence to recruit. It is illegal to trade as a recruitment agency with being licensed by the Department of Jobs, Enterprise & Innovation and using an unlicensed agency leaves you with no avenue of redress if things go wrong.

- Check whether the agency is registered with the National Recruitment Federation.[3]

- Check whether the agency operates in your market(s) / industry sector(s).

- Check how much the agency's staff know about your organisation.

- Review and agree the terms and conditions in detail before the recruitment begins.

- Check the small print for clawback clauses and for ownership of candidates (where potential candidates are referred by more than one agency). Ensure there are claw-backs included for your organisation also, where employees leave or have their employment terminated within six months of starting.

If you are planning on further recruitment or recruiting for more than one role, consider tendering the work to more than one agency and invite

---

[3]   The National Recruitment Federation (**www.nrf.ie**) is a voluntary body that establishes and maintains standards for the recruitment industry. It has developed a Certificate in Recruitment Practice (with Institute of Leadership & Management and City & Guilds), currently the only dedicated course of its kind in Ireland.

them to pitch to your organisation – this way you are guaranteed to have competitive quotations for the role.

The process of working with a recruitment agency is:

- Meet with the successful agency and specifically with the consultant who is going to look after you / your organisation.
- Take time to update the agency on your organisation, its background and activities and how this role fits into the overall organisation structure.
- Provide the recruitment consultant with the detailed job specification.
- Discuss broadly the remuneration package with the recruitment consultant, as the detailed package will be negotiated later on if the agency provides you with a successful candidate – they will want the highest salary negotiable for their candidates, since their commission depends on it.
- Agree a timeline in which you expect to receive applications.
- Agree whether you want the agency to shortlist before sending you applications.
- When you have received the applications, ensure a quick turnaround and give feedback on why you have selected the candidates for the next round in the process.
- Agree dates for the next stage of the process with the agency and follow up with all candidates.
- Interview candidates.
- Provide feedback to the recruitment consultant / agency on successful and unsuccessful candidates.
- Agree with the recruitment consultant which of you will decline and offer candidates in the next step of the process.
- Communicate a verbal offer to the recruitment consultant/ candidate as agreed.
- Agree the remuneration and high level terms and conditions.

- Issue a letter of offer, conditional on satisfactory references and / or medical checks.

- Agree a start date for the new employee.

- Pay agency after employee has started, ensuring first that, if the employee should leave prematurely or have their employment terminated, your organisation will be reimbursed by the agency.

See also
Q16 What are the best ways to recruit?
Q18 What is headhunting?
Q31 Should a job offer be subject to a satisfactory reference check?
Q32 Should a job offer be subject to a medical examination?

Q20   How do we know we have shortlisted the right candidates?

Screening and shortlisting candidates is a process by which applications are reviewed against the criteria set out for the role.

Screening candidates is the process of reviewing all CVs and applications against the original job specification, advertisement or agreed criteria. Candidates who do not meet the criteria will be ruled out and will not progress to the next stage in the selection process (shortlisting).

Shortlisting involves marking the remaining candidates relative to one another, to identify the candidates to bring to the next stage in the process.

Large organisations often use online mechanisms to screen applications – particularly at lower level, entry-type roles, where the competencies are clear, and a simple "Yes" or "No" might screen someone in or out of the process.

Most organisations also use application forms to standardise the application process and to help with continuity and overall objectivity.

Shortlisting candidates for the next stage of the process must be fair and transparent – especially since candidates could come back at a later stage and request to see the shortlisting that screened them out of the process.

Therefore, screening and shortlisting should:

- Have pre-agreed criteria for assessing applications against the details of the vacancy.
- Have a rating system, whereby only candidates who meet the agreed criteria move on to the next stage of the process.
- Ensure compliance with all equality legislation and that candidates are screened out only for a valid reason.
- Have more than one person involved.
- Include regular and continuous review of the process to ensure that it is fair and transparent.

See also

Q21 Interviewing – is there a right way / best practice?

Q26 Are there techniques, other than interviewing, that would help us to choose the right candidate?

Q21   Interviewing – is there a right way / best practice?

There are a number of different ways to interview candidates, and many different techniques may be used. In all cases, however, the interviewer should:

- Ensure the candidate knows what type of interview it is, and is aware of the type of questioning that will be used.
- Introduce everyone present at the interview and alert the candidate to your need to take notes, which might lead to occasional loss of eye contact.
- Agree in advance with the other interviewers the questions (and the types of answers you would expect to hear).
- Ask one question at a time.
- Ask the questions you want to ask, not just those you think you should (being mindful of anything that might be discriminatory).
- Remember the 80/20 rule! Don't talk too much ... you are the interviewer not the interviewee.
- Listen to the interviewee's answers carefully.
- Ensure that all candidates (for the same role) are asked the same questions

There are certain areas that should also be avoided during an interview. Interviewers should not:

- Ask age-related questions.
- Ask a candidate whether they have children, and if so how might the children be looked after if the candidate is successful in obtaining the role.
- Ask a disabled person how they might perform certain parts of the role if they were successful in obtaining the role.
- Ask a woman something that would never be asked of a man or *vice versa*!

To avoid any of these pitfalls, ask the same questions of all candidates, and ensure that you (and anyone interviewing with you) are aware of the requirements of the equality legislation and its implications.

See also
Q20   How do we know we have shortlisted the right candidates?
Q26   Are there techniques, other than interviewing, that would help us to choose the right candidate?
Q29   How do we protect ourselves from claims of bias or discrimination from unsuccessful candidates?

QUICK WIN LEADERSHIP, Q70 How can I use the interview process more effectively to help me find the best people for my team?

Q22   Who should interview candidates?

Interviewers play a key role in the selection process. If only one person meets with the candidate, the result is likely to be a much more informal interview than when the candidate faces a panel. However, a panel interview, while potentially unwieldy, gives objectivity to the process and can reduce the need for further interviews.

In all cases, interviewers should be:

- Familiar with the role.
- Prepared for the interview by having reviewed each of the shortlisted candidates' applications in detail.
- Ideally, skilled at interviewing.

There should be at least two people on an interview panel, and ideally three. The best mix is a representative from the business unit the candidate is likely to work in – ideally, the prospective line manager; a representative from another business unit in the organisation, from a talent and succession perspective; and a representative from HR to give objective advice.

It is good practice to ensure an interviewer panel comprises interviewers of both genders. And, if you are interviewing in Northern Ireland, it may be sensible to ensure a mix of religious perspectives.

See also
Q21   Interviewing – is there a right way / best practice?
Q29   How do we protect ourselves from claims of bias or discrimination from unsuccessful candidates?

Q23 How do we assess candidates at interview?

There are a number of ways of assessing candidates at interview. Common interview approaches include:

- Biographical interviews.
- Competency-based interviews.

Biographical interviews are the traditional interview, in which the interviewer asks questions relating to the candidate's experiences as outlined in their CV.

Interviewers need to be particularly skilled at interviewing to have success with this type of interview, as it can lose direction and does not always result in achieving the answers that the interviewer was trying to solicit. However, due to their familiarity, biographical interviews can put candidates at ease.

Interviewers should have a checklist of skills, abilities and personal traits, weighted in terms of what is important to the organisation and the role, so that they can rate these during the course of the interview. The checklist might include:

- Relevant work experience.
- General intelligence.
- Disposition.
- Team or individual player – will they fit into your team?
- How the candidate presents themselves – physically and verbally.
- Educational background – is it what you are looking for? Which are desirable or required elements?
- Candidates' expectations – can the organisation support them?

Competency-based interviews are a more structured approach to interviewing, and leave little room for the candidate to pretend they have more experience than they actually do. Every candidate is asked the same questions, based on the competencies as outlined in the job description. Normally, the candidates are given these competencies before the interview to allow them time to prepare. The questions should ask for specific examples of the candidate's experience – for example:

- "Give me an example of a time when you were faced with a difficult situation and you had to influence someone in authority ...?" The competency tested here is the candidate's influencing skills. The candidate must have had that experience in order to answer that question effectively.

Competency-based interviews also have a strict marking system whereby the criteria and weighting are agreed beforehand and candidates are scored against the criteria over the course of the interview.

At the end of the interviews, the interviewers present their scores to each other for discussion and debate, and ultimately selection of the candidate(s) for the next stage in the recruitment process. It is essential that the scoring and rating system is objective and defensible, with as little subjectivity as possible.

All interviewers should ensure that their interview notes, scores and ratings are legible and rational, as these records must be kept in case of later query by candidates, successful or unsuccessful.

See also
Q21   Interviewing – is there a right way / best practice?
Q27   How do we know we have chosen the right person after the interview process?
Q28   What records do we need to keep of the interview process?
Q29   How do we protect ourselves from claims of bias or discrimination from unsuccessful candidates?

Q24   How do we plan for an interview?

When the candidates have been shortlisted, the next step is to arrange the interviews. Most likely, candidates will be attending the interview at your organisation's premises, so this is an opportunity to market your organisation and its employer brand. A candidate's first impression or their overall experience during the selection process is one of the key factors in their decision to accept or decline an offer to join your organisation.

When preparing for the interview:

- Notify candidates in plenty of time that they have been shortlisted and are called for interview.
- Communicate clearly with the candidate the time, date and venue of the interview and who they should ask for on their arrival.
- Try to accommodate the candidate if there is an issue with the time offered for interview (perhaps they are coming from their current place of work to the interview).
- Communicate clearly with the candidate the type of interview it will be (competency-based), and what preparations (if any) they should make beforehand.
- Ensure that the candidate does not wait too long for their interview – this shows a lack of concern for them. However, if there is a legitimate reason for a delay, update the candidate.
- Ensure the room for the interview is well-planned – avoid any sense of an 'interrogation'.
- Make sure there is drinking water available for the candidate.

When preparing yourself as an interviewer:

- Meet with the other interviewers well in advance of the interview, and agree who will take the lead role in introducing the panel and what questions will be asked by whom.
- Agree the weightings and the rating system.

- Leave plenty of time for the scoring discussions at the end of the session.

The interview pack
Each interviewer should have an interview pack, which should include:

- The original job advertisement and job specification.
- The candidates' CVs or applications (or both).
- Any other relevant information.
- Prepared, relevant to-the-job (agreed) questions.
- Interviewers' marking sheets.

And make sure that interviewers have plenty of extra pens and paper to take detailed notes – there is nothing as disconcerting as an interviewer looking for peens or paper and appearing much unprepared, when the candidate is expected to be very prepared.

The interview
For the interview itself:

- Decide on the length of time for each interview.
- Allow time between interviews for over-runs and for discussion between interviewers.
- Aim to complete no more than six to eight interviews in one day – more than this and it becomes difficult to remember individual candidates.

See also
Q21 Interviewing – is there a right way / best practice?
Q22 Who should interview candidates?
Q23 How do we assess candidates at interview?
Q25 How do we conduct an interview?

Q25 How do we conduct an interview?

There are essentially three stages to any interview:

- **The opening / introduction:** This part of the interview introduces the candidate to the panel and their roles within the organisation. The interviewers may offer the candidate some water and put the candidate at ease. The interviewers also can explain the structure of the interview, how it will progress, that notes will be taken and, if it is a competency-based interview, that it will be very structured by way of questions from that point on.

- **The interview itself:** This forms the major part of the interview, allowing the interviewers to question the candidate on their CV / application against the set criteria and job description.

- **The close:** This offers the candidate an opportunity to ask any questions they might have, and for the interviewers to update the candidate on the next steps in the process.

To avoid pitfalls, ask the same questions of all candidates, and ensure that you (and anyone interviewing with you) are fully aware of the requirements of the equality legislation and its implications.

See also
Q21 Interviewing – is there a right way / best practice?
Q22 Who should interview candidates?
Q23 How do we assess candidates at interview?
Q24 How do we plan for an interview?

Q26   Are there techniques, other than interviewing, that would help us to choose the right candidate?

A wide range of other techniques are used to assess candidates other than interviewing, although many of them often are used in conjunction with interviewing.

The more common recruitment techniques used are:

- Assessment centres.
- Presentations.
- Role plays.
- In-tray exercises.
- Psychometric testing.

Assessment centres normally are run over the course of no less than one day, during which a group of assessors (usually, four to six) test all candidates at different times on a battery of tests, exercises and activities, including:

- Psychometric and personality tests.
- Competency-based interviews.
- Case-studies.
- Presentations.
- Role plays.
- Group interactions.

At the end of the day, all the scores from the assessors are added up and the candidate(s) with the best score(s) goes to the next stage of the process. Assessment centres often are used in graduate recruitment, where the candidates are less experienced and the centre is used to assess their potential.

Presentations are used in many different ways in the recruitment process:

- Candidates may be given a case-study in advance and asked to prepare a presentation for delivery at the interview or assessment centre (this allows the interviewers / assessors to review a candidate's ability to research and present on a topic).

- Candidates may be given a case study on the day and given some (not much) time to prepare a presentation – (this allows interviewers / assessors to review a candidate's ability both to think on their feet and to present).

- Candidates (particularly for senior roles leading teams) may be asked to present on their plan for the organisation – for example, a 30, 60 or 90-day plan (this allows the interviewers to review both a candidate's ability to present and to develop a blueprint for the organisation should they be successful in obtaining the role).

Role plays give interviewers / assessors the opportunity to see how the candidate might behave in their new role, although some HR professionals believe role plays give an advantage to candidates with good presenting or acting skills.

In-tray exercises can be very successful, especially for very detailed administrative or secretarial roles. Candidates are asked to review an in-tray where there will be urgent, important and not important material. There may also be an exercise in working with spreadsheets and / or letters. This type of exercise usually provides concrete evidence for interviewers' / assessors' decisions, since candidates' proficiency is clearly demonstrated (or not, as the case may be).

Psychometric tests are used to provide an objective means of measuring a person's knowledge, characteristics and abilities and attitudes. They are rarely used on their own in the recruitment process.

In overall terms, you must decide what bests suits your organisation when assessing candidates, taking into account:

- Time away from their own responsibilities for interviewers / assessors.
- Candidates' time availability.
- Costs.

The common denominator in choosing a selection method in most organisations is the desire to meet potential new employees face-to-face, so interviews are almost inevitable. On that basis, since competency-based interviews are more objective than biographical interviews, they are a better option!

See also
Q20   How do we know we have shortlisted the right candidates?
Q21   Interviewing – is there a right way / best practice?
Q27   How do we know we have chosen the right person after the interview process?

QUICK WIN LEADERSHIP, Q71   What other tools can I use to help me select the best employees?

Q27   How do we know we have chosen the right person after the interview process?

It is difficult to be absolutely sure that you have chosen the right person for the role until they have been working in the role for a period of time.

However, if during the recruitment process, you:

- Ensured you had a detailed job specification and person specification (signed off by the line manager(s));
- Sourced a mix of best-in-market candidates;
- Are satisfied that you conducted well-prepared, detailed, objective and balanced interviews (and other assessments, as appropriate); and
- Reference-checked thoroughly your successful candidate;

you should be satisfied that you have done everything possible to ensure a successful outcome.

Nonetheless, it is worthwhile considering giving your organisation an opt-out clause – should something come to light before the employee starts work – by making your letter of offer conditional on a number of points:

- Satisfactory reference checks.
- Copies of performance reviews.
- Original certificates for degrees and other certificates.
- A medical examination.

In addition, it is also worth considering including a probationary period in the new employee's written statement of terms of employment (contract). This gives the organisation time to assess the employee's actual performance on the job before making them permanent in the role.

See also
Q20   How do we know we have shortlisted the right candidates?

Q21   Interviewing – is there a right way / best practice?
Q26   Are there techniques, other than interviewing, that would help us to choose the right candidate?
Q31   Should a job offer be subject to a satisfactory reference check?
Q32   Should a job offer be subject to a medical examination?
Q38   What is probation –and how does it work?

Q28 What records do we need to keep of the interview process?

It is critical that an organisation's interview records are kept on file for at least 12 months after the interviews have taken place. As an employer, you may be required at any point to produce these records, particularly where there may be a claim from an unsuccessful candidate.

Interviews should be well-structured and documented and all the relevant details of that process kept on file. **Q24** outlined the interview pack that interviewers should have when interviewing candidates. When this documentation is completed at the end of the interview process, all the interviewers' records should be kept together and filed. The information that typically should be kept includes:

- Job description.
- Person specification.
- The vacancy or advertisement.
- The interview assessment sheets and how the ratings and weightings were agreed.
- All notes relating to the interview.

See also
Q24 How do we plan for an interview?
Q29 How do we protect ourselves from claims of bias or discrimination from unsuccessful candidates?

Q29　How do we protect ourselves from claims of bias or discrimination from unsuccessful candidates?

If a candidate is unsuccessful in securing a role in your organisation, and feels aggrieved in terms of how the recruitment or interview process was conducted, they have up to 12 months (after the date of the alleged discrimination) to bring a claim alleging discrimination. It is imperative, therefore, not only in terms of best practice but from a compliance perspective that your organisation is very clear about the legislation in this regard.

In Ireland where claims are made by employees, the Equality Tribunal reviews the process and the documentation provided by both parties. The fairness and transparency of the process is a key factor in deciding whether there is a claim or not.

In large organisations, where there has been high volume recruitment, ensuring that all processes are strictly adhered to can be a challenge, particularly where there is an urgency to recruit and the timelines are tight. However, the use of more sophisticated candidate management systems can ensure that the relevant details relating to the interview process are held in a central database, assuming they have been input correctly.

In smaller organisations, where the introduction of such systems is not feasible, the only way to ensure compliance is to have a clear, practical, documented recruitment process, signed off by management, which is continuously reviewed. Ideally, if there is a central HR department, all interview records should be stored centrally under the job vacancy and a copy of the successful candidate's interview notes kept on their HR file also.

See also
Q28　What records do we need to keep of the interview process?

Q30 How do we make a job offer?

How you sourced the candidate initially determines how you make a job offer to them:

- If the candidate was sourced through a head-hunter, the headhunter normally makes the job offer on behalf of your organisation.
- If the candidate was sourced through a recruitment agency, either you or the agency can make the offer – decide in advance who does it.
- If the candidate has been sourced in any other way, normally the organisation makes the offer to the candidate.

The best way to make an offer to a successful candidate is face-to-face. Invite the candidate to meet with you and congratulate them on getting the job. Offer them the role verbally at this point and outline the key terms and conditions. If it is not possible to meet face-to-face, make the offer over the phone but always speak with the candidate directly – don't leave messages. Then:

- Ask the candidate whether they have any questions.
- Agree a date / time for the candidate to revert to you with an answer on accepting the offer.

Follow up with a letter of offer (by email) in the interim confirming your discussion and including all the relevant terms and conditions, including an expiry date on the offer (not a statutory inclusion), and asking the employee to return a signed copy to your organisation.

Unsuccessful candidates should be declined in writing at this point.

See also
Q31 Should a job offer be subject to a satisfactory reference check?
Q32 Should a job offer be subject to a medical examination?

Q31   Should a job offer be subject to a satisfactory reference check?

Many organisations offer employment subject to a satisfactory reference check. The reason for this is so that organisations can verify that what has been said at interview is accurate and a true reflection of the candidate's presentation of themselves.

Ideally, reference checks should be done face-to-face, although often this is not possible – particularly in large organisations where there are many references to be checked out and verified. Some organisations, due to the volume of recruitment, outsource reference checking to a third party.

Reference checks, whether outsourced or not, should include confirmation of the following (not exhaustive):

- That the candidate worked for the organisation stated.
- The dates they were employed.
- Their last working relationship.
- The role the candidate held while employed there
- Their rate of pay.
- Their attendance (or absenteeism).
- Their performance (good and bad).
- Their disciplinary record.
- Their reason for leaving.
- The previous organisation's willingness to re-employ the candidate.
- Any other comments on the candidate generally.

It is important that reference checks are completed as quickly as possible after the letter of offer has been sent – and certainly before the successful candidate starts work with your organisation. Otherwise, if they start work and are settling in well, and then the reference check raises an issue of concern, it may be quite tricky at that point to extricate them.

See also
Q30   How do we make a job offer?
Q32   Should a job offer be subject to a medical examination?

Q32 Should a job offer be subject to a medical examination?

Most companies ensure that some sort of medical examination is carried out, or in some cases a pre-employment medical questionnaire is completed, before employing a person.

It is always better to ensure that medical examinations or questionnaires are offered before employment starts, and in most cases the offer of employment is conditional on passing a medical examination.

Normally, the prospective employer pays for the medical examination, and also has the results forwarded to the organisation (this must be agreed with the candidate).

Pre-employment questionnaire

A pre-employment questionnaire is usually about one page in length and essentially asks the candidate to answer a number of health-related questions. Normally, it also asks the candidate for permission to contact the candidate's own doctor should it be warranted at any point.

The questionnaire also states that the job offer is conditional on satisfactory completion of the questionnaire and that any aspect may be verified with their own doctor.

Medical examinations

It is important to ensure compliance with equality legislation when medical examinations are being carried out – for example, a woman who is pregnant should not be treated any differently or less favourably than a man.

Also if the medical examination is carried out and it shows that the candidate has a disability, the organisation must have clear evidence to show that the person would not be able to perform in the role as a result of this disability, in order to withdraw any job offer – especially since it is a legal requirement for organisations to do all that is reasonable to accommodate those with a disability.

See also
Q29 How do we protect ourselves from claims of bias or discrimination from unsuccessful candidates?
Q30 How do we make a job offer?
Q31 Should a job offer be subject to a satisfactory reference check?

Q33   What do we do if we cannot identify suitable candidates in Ireland and want to recruit from outside Ireland?

Recruiting from outside Ireland was prevalent over the last number of years, but has become less common in the current downturn. That said, if an organisation wants to recruit outside Ireland, it is possible.

The EU and EEA (the EU states combined with Iceland, Norway and Liechtenstein) allow free movement of labour between member states without an employment permit. However, if an Irish organisation wishes to employ a non-EEA person, then it must apply for a work permit for that person.

Recruiting from outside Ireland is easier than it used to be with the introduction of social media and online job boards. Candidates are more mobile and often commute to work in Ireland on a weekly / monthly basis from other countries.

Agencies that specialise in recruiting from outside Ireland can arrange everything from sourcing, interviewing and issuing a contract to an employee to meeting and settling them into their new accommodation arrival. This makes recruiting very easy for the organisation – the downside is that sometimes the organisation does not have a real input into the selection of the candidate, which is not ideal.

When recruiting from outside Ireland:

- Have a clear, detailed well thought-out job description.
- Decide whether the remuneration package will be an 'ex-pat' package or at regular recruitment rates?
- Ensure you are advertising in the right markets.
- Communicate clearly with the candidate on what expenses will be paid during the recruitment process.
- Communicate the likely recruitment process from the outset in terms of timelines and the potential need for availability.

- Conduct initial interviews by phone or internet (Skype) to reduce cost.

- Ensure candidates are eligible to work in Ireland.

- If candidates are travelling from another country for interview, ensure they have all the travel details beforehand and are not too tired for the interview when they arrive.

- If the candidate is successful and is likely to commute for the role, ensure they take appropriate advice in terms of currencies and tax.

See also
Q8 What are the key steps in the recruitment process?
Q12 How do we establish a fair remuneration package for a specific job?

Q34   How do we manage a recruitment freeze?

Recruitment freezes are commonplace now both in the private and public sectors. The key challenge for organisations when they freeze recruitment always is how to manage the expectations of stakeholders during these times. Inevitably, the decision to freeze recruitment is taken at the top, at Board level, which is appropriate. However, the communication after that is not always as clear cut; often senior managers do not want to share bad news with their teams and, with competing priorities, they simply 'forget'.

The following pointers may be helpful for recruitment and HR teams in managing expectations of all concerned, when faced with a recruitment freeze:

- Keep communication lines open with the business units and do not hide behind emails.
- Agree and publish where and when the freeze starts – for example, if the organisation is in discussion with a candidate, at what point is it acceptable to withdraw?
- Ensure the freeze is not used as an excuse to not hire a candidate who already has a contract and is starting next week!
- Agree an escalation process for your team, in exceptional circumstances.
- Ensure that recruitment administration is 100% accurate (zero tolerance) – this is crucial – for example, where a Department Head wants to step outside of the freeze, ensure the same process applies to them even if they say otherwise!
- Ensure you fully support your team and, where appropriate, step in.
- Where line managers are unsure of the process, reissue the process with follow-up meetings.

The other HR challenge posed by a recruitment freeze – 'defrosting' – is more straightforward: only start to defrost when it has been categorically agreed with the organisation's leadership (in writing, if necessary).

Defrosting recruitment may start with some support from a flexible workforce option – for example, there may be an opportunity to:

- Recruit temporary staff initially.
- Recruit contract staff initially.
- Restructure internally.

HR should provide options for the organisation once it starts to recruit again. Consider your recruitment strategies before the need arises.

See also

Q2   How do we establish our staffing needs?
Q30   How do we make a job offer?
Q35   What type of employment contract should we offer?
Q74   How can interns / work placements help us cope with sudden changes in staffing needs?
Q96   We are restructuring our business – where do we start?

Q35   What type of employment contract should we offer?

Once an offer of employment has been made, an employee must be given a written statement of terms of employment within two months of the commencement of their employment. The type of contract to offer is up to the organisation, and should be decided before recruitment begins.

Types of employment contracts include:

- Full-time contract / contract of indefinite duration.
- Part-time contract.
- Job-sharing contract.
- Temporary contract:
  - Fixed term contract.
  - Contract for a specified purpose.
- Zero hour contract.

A contract of indefinite duration (employees often mistakenly refer to this type of contract as a 'permanent contract') is the most common and familiar form of employment contract. Indefinite duration means there is no end date on the contract unless retirement is reached.

A part-time contract is used where a role has fewer hours (per week / month / year) than a contract of indefinite duration.

A job-sharing contract is used where one role is shared between two (commonly) or maybe more people. It is agreed with the job-sharers what hours should be worked (often week on, week off, alternating the weeks) and how the work is completed.

A temporary contract, unlike an indefinite duration or part-time contract, has an end date – either a fixed end date (fixed term contract), or when the project ends (specified purpose).

A zero hour contract is used where an employee is required to be available for work (perhaps to cover in an emergency) without the guarantee of work. Alternatively, the employee may be asked to be available for work on a specified day or days, although the exact number of hours of work available is not specified. Compensation is payable even when the employee is not working but has been required to make themselves available over a period without the guarantee of work.

See also
Q30   How do we make a job offer?
Q36   What must we include in an employment contract?
Q37   Does an employment contract have to be a written contract to be legally binding?

Q36   What must we include in an employment contract?

An employment contract (or a written statement of terms of employment) must be issued to a new employee within two months of starting their new employment. It should include the following:

- The full names of both the employer (the legal employing entity) and the employee to whom the contract is being issued.
- The address of the employer – the address at which the employer is based or the registered address.
- Job title of the (new) role, and the purpose of the role within the organisation.
- The date of commencement of the role.
- Location – where the employee will be based for the purposes of the employment, which may be different to the registered address of the employer.
- Hours of work, including any reference to overtime.
- Salary – the payment due to the employee for the hours worked and how this is calculated.
- Payment of salary – how the salary is to be paid – monthly, weekly or daily.
- Leave – any reference to paid leave (annual leave, etc).
- Sick leave – any reference to paid sick leave.
- Pensions – any schemes for which the employee may be eligible.
- Notice periods – periods of notice due from both the employer and employee outside of any redundancy notice.
- Trade unions – reference made to any agreements that may affect the employee's terms and conditions.

The contract should be signed and dated by both the employer and the employee. It is not a statutory requirement for the employee to sign the employment contract although it is best practice for them to do so.

Usually, the employer provides two copies for signing, keeps one and gives the other to the employee for their own records.

See also

Q11 What should be included in a remuneration package?

Q12 How do we establish a fair remuneration package for a specific job?

Q35 What type of employment contract should we offer?

Q37 Does an employment contract have to be a written contract to be legally binding?

Q43 How many days annual leave are employees entitled to?

Q44 What public holidays are employees entitled to?

Q46 How should we respond to an employee who requests time off for jury service?

Q47 What are female employees' entitlements to maternity leave?

Q48 What are female employees' entitlements on their return to work after maternity leave?

Q49 What are male employees' entitlements to paternity leave?

Q50 Can both parents take parental leave?

Q51 What are employees' entitlements to adoptive leave?

Q52 What are employees' entitlements to carers' leave?

Q53 Who is entitled to sick pay – and for how long?

Q54 What compassionate leave should we allow employees?

Q72 Can we prevent employees from joining a trade union?

Q82 What pension rights do employees have?

Q83 On what grounds can we terminate an employee's contract?

Q84 When is it legal to terminate without a notice period?

Q91 Must all employees serve out their notice period?

Q37   Does an employment contract have to be a written contract to be legally binding?

There are three ways by which a contract may be formed:

- Express written agreement.
- Express oral agreement.
- Conduct of the parties – this means that, although not expressed, the terms of a contract can be held to exist because of the conduct of the parties and custom and practice.

Two principles govern the formation of a contract:

- **Offer:** There must be a clear and specific offer of employment by the employer to the prospective employee. It is advisable from the employer's point of view that all conditions attached to a job offer are clarified with, and understood by, the prospective employee, before a firm offer is made in writing.

- **Acceptance:** A contract for employment comes into existence once acceptance is formally indicated. It is important to note the time of acceptance as the offer may be withdrawn at any time before – but not after – it is accepted, preferably in writing. The benefit of requiring a clear acceptance by the employee is that this establishes a firm documented basis for the contractual relationship.

Thus almost every employee has a contract of employment, although it may not be expressly written!

See also
Q35   What type of employment contract should we offer?
Q36   What must we include in an employment contract?

Q38   What is probation –and how does it work?

Probation allows an organisation to review an employee's actual performance for a period after she or he starts work, before making the employee permanent in the role. A probationary period must be included in the employee's written statement of terms of employment (contract).

During the probationary period, the line manager should assess the employee's performance in line with the objectives set and agreed with the employee. It is essential that the employee is given regular, structured and documented feedback on their performance.

If the employee is not meeting their objectives, the organisation may extend the probationary period. If, at the end of the extension, the employee is still not performing, then the organisation may choose not to make the employee permanent in the role but to let them go instead.

A probationary period commonly is for six months, but may be for any period up to 12 months, at which stage the Unfair Dismissals legislation applies.

See also
Q60   What is performance appraisal?
Q61   When and how should we introduce performance appraisal?
Q64   How do we deal with underperformance by an employee?
Q83   On what grounds can we terminate an employee's contract?

Q39   Do we need an induction programme?

An induction programme is the employee's first formal introduction to company as an employee, and shows them 'how things are done around here'. The programme is a practical way of sharing information with them and of ensuring that they are fully aware of (and sign off on) their responsibilities within the organisation.

Induction programmes can be very powerful and positive experiences for employees and are recognised as assisting in reducing turnover. The first three months of an employee's tenure with an organisation is usually when their decision to stay or leave is made. If an employee experiences a positive induction and is given time to settle in, this is often rewarded with a decision to stay and a determination to perform well.

In large organisations, there may be more than one induction programme – there may be an organisation-level presentation followed by a local business unit-level induction for those employees joining that specific department.

In smaller organisations, there is normally just one induction programme scheduled a few times a year, which covers all aspects of the business and includes all new hires, whether or not they will be working together.

One of the most important factors in introducing an induction programme is to ensure that it has senior management support. The best induction programmes always have senior management in attendance, and they normally open the induction programme.

See also
Q5   How do we identify what training employees need?
Q6   What should be included in an employee handbook?
Q7   How do we communicate our employee handbook and its contents to employees?

QUICK WIN LEADERSHIP, Q72 Why is employee induction so important to maintaining a team dynamic?

Q40 What should we include in an induction programme?

An induction programme can cover many topics and, in some companies can take up to eight weeks, including training. Commonly though, induction takes two to three days and covers housekeeping, operational and legal issues.

Ideally, the induction programme should be opened by the most senior person in the organisation available.

Housekeeping matters might include:

- How to enter the building – including security arrangements for out-of-hours working.
- Where to have lunch and or breaks (where the canteen is, if there is one).
- Where the various other facilities are.

Operational matters might include:

- An overview of the organisation and its goals.
- An introduction to the management team.
- Where the employee's role fits in the overall organisation.
- Presentations on different aspects of the business.

Legal matters might include:

- Conditions of employment.
- Policies and procedures – for example, on email and internet use, or bullying and harassment.
- Health and safety requirements.
- Grievance and disciplinary procedures.

See also
Q5   How do we identify what training employees need?
Q6   What should be included in an employee handbook?

Q7   How do we communicate our employee handbook and its contents to employees?

Q36   What must we include in an employment contract?

Q57   What responsibilities do we have, as an employer, for health and safety?

Q58   What responsibilities do employees have for health and safety?

Q66   What should be included in our grievance and disciplinary policies?

Q67   What should be included in our grievance procedure?

Q68   What should be included in our disciplinary procedure?

Q69   What should be included in our disciplinary appeals procedure?

Q79   Should we have a data protection policy?

Q80   What do we do if an employee claims he / she is being bullied or harassed?

Q81   What should be included in an email policy?

Q41 What records do we need to hold on our employees?

An employee's file should include a number of basic documents that are fundamental to their role within the organisation:

- The written statement of terms of employment (contract).
- Their application / CV.
- The interview assessment form, documents and all related notes.
- Their personal details, including PPS number, name, address and all relevant details.
- Medical examination results.
- References.
- Signed acknowledgement of all induction details – for example, understanding of health and safety policy, grievance and disciplinary policies and procedures, etc.
- All documents relating to their probationary period.
- All performance review details and documents.
- Notes of verbal warnings and copies of written warnings given under the organisation's disciplinary procedures.
- Details of any awards or commendations given to, or won y, the employee.
- Details of salary increases awarded to the employee.

These records should be kept up-to-date and retained for an appropriate period after the employee's retirement, resignation or dismissal.

See also
Q7   How do we communicate our employee handbook and its contents to employees?
Q28   What records do we need to keep of the interview process?
Q31   Should a job offer be subject to a satisfactory reference check?

Q32 Should a job offer be subject to a medical examination?

Q38 What is probation –and how does it work?

Q42 What information can we hold on unsuccessful candidates – and for how long?

Q60 What is performance appraisal?

Q64 How do we deal with underperformance by an employee?

Q66 What should be included in our grievance and disciplinary policies?

Q67 What should be included in our grievance procedure?

Q68 What should be included in our disciplinary procedure?

Q42   What information can we hold on unsuccessful candidates – and for how long?

Like all records relating to the interview and recruitment process, it is important to hold information on unsuccessful candidates, just as you would for successful candidates. Experience HR practitioners argue that holding information on unsuccessful candidates is more important, as they are more likely to take a claim against the organisation if they feel aggrieved and believe they should have got the job. The timeframe for such a claim is up to 12 months.

There is no requirement to keep any other documentation on unsuccessful candidates other than the information and documentation relating their recruitment and interview process.

See also
Q28   What records do we need to keep of the interview process?
Q29   How do we protect ourselves from claims of bias or discrimination from unsuccessful candidates?
Q41   What records do we need to hold on our employees?

DURING EMPLOYMENT

Q43   How many days annual leave are employees entitled to?

The minimum statutory annual leave entitlements for employees are:

- Four working weeks (20 days) in a leave year for employees who work at least 1,365 hours a year.
- One-third of a working week per calendar month where the employee works at least 117 hours in the month.
- 8% of the hours worked by a part-time employee in a leave year. Their maximum entitlement is four weeks of the part-time person's working weeks.

There is no qualifying period for annual leave. All employees are entitled to annual leave.

Many organisations offer more leave than the statutory entitlement to employees as part of an employee's overall benefit package.

See also
Q11   What should be included in a remuneration package?
Q44   What public holidays are employees entitled to?
Q45   Are all employees entitled to company days?

Q44   What public holidays are employees entitled to?

The statutory public holidays in Ireland are:

- New Year's Day, 1 January.
- St. Patrick's Day, 17 March.
- Easter Monday.
- The first Monday in May.
- The first Monday in June.
- The first Monday in August.
- The last Monday in October.
- Christmas Day, 25 December.
- St Stephen's Day, 26 December.

Public holidays and 'bank holidays' are often confused, with many people believing they are the same thing (which they are not) and using the terms interchangeably. Bank holidays, such as Good Friday and Christmas Eve, are traditionally days when banks and other financial institutions are closed. The decision to close on these days and to release staff is an organisational decision and not a statutory entitlement.

For the purposes of fulfilling statutory public holiday obligations, an employer may substitute specified religious holidays for certain public holidays. The employer must give 14 days' advance notice of any such change.

Importantly, an employee is entitled to the following in respect of public holidays:

- A paid day off on the day, or
- An additional day of annual leave, or
- A paid day off within a month of that day, or
- An additional day's pay.

Finally and importantly, there is no qualifying period of service for an entitlement to public holidays.

See also

Q43   How many days annual leave are employees entitled to?

Q45   Are all employees entitled to company days?

Q45 Are all employees entitled to company days?

Company days are not statutory leave.

Some organisations request that some of their employees' annual leave entitlement is taken on days specified by the organisation ('company days') in order to support the organisation's requirements. For example, a large plant might close for maintenance for two weeks in the summer, during which time virtually all staff would take annual leave or an organisation might ask staff to take one or more days' leave in the Christmas / New Year period.

See also
Q44 What public holidays are employees entitled to?

Q46   How should we respond to an employee who requests time off for jury service?

Jury service is a statutory leave entitlement for everyone who is on the electoral register. To be called for jury service means to attend a court and potentially be called as a jury member in any given day.

Some people are excluded from jury service – those connected to the law in Ireland: solicitors, the Gardaí, and the Defence Forces – and others may be excluded – those who may be incapable of doing their jury service, or those who provide a religious or other valid reason for not attending.

However, if someone fails to give a reasonable excuse and does not attend jury service, they can be fined.

If an employee requests time off for jury leave, the organisation should reserve the right to request a certificate of jury service to obtain proof whether the individual has served on a jury previously.

As it is a constitutional right for an employee to attend for jury service, they must be allowed to attend and must be paid by the organisation while on jury service.

If an employee is released from jury service, they should be expected to return to work immediately.

Q47 What are female employees' entitlements to maternity leave?

If a female employee is expecting a baby, she is entitled to a continuous period of 26 weeks' maternity leave around the time of birth of the child. She maintains all of her employee rights (other than remuneration) during this 26-week period, including a full entitlement to annual leave and public holidays. Of the 26-week period, at least two weeks must be taken before the expected date of birth, and at least four after the birth.

Once the pregnancy is confirmed, the employee is required to advise the organisation in writing as soon as possible and at least four weeks before the commencement of her maternity leave. This notice must be accompanied by a doctor's certificate stating the expected date of birth, and a note from her explaining whether she intends to return to work.

She also may take up to 16 weeks in additional maternity leave at the end of the statutory 26-week period, if she wishes. A female employee should apply in writing for this leave at least four weeks before her maternity leave expires.

When maternity leave ends, she is entitled to return to her usual job in so far as it is reasonably practical. However, if this is not possible, she should be offered suitable alternative work. She also must provide the organisation with at least four weeks' notice of her intention to return to work and her planned date of return.

Pay during maternity leave

While female employees are on maternity leave, they normally are entitled to payment from the Department of Social Protection for the 26 weeks' maternity leave, depending on meeting certain Pay Related Social Insurance (PRSI) eligibility criteria. Social Welfare benefits are not payable during the optional additional 16 weeks' maternity leave.

For an employee to get the full maternity benefit entitlement, she must provide a minimum of four weeks' written notice of her intention to take maternity leave, and again four weeks' written notice of her intention to take additional maternity leave.

There is no requirement on an employer to pay a female employee during maternity leave – statutory or additional. However, many so, making up any difference between maternity benefit and the employee's normal take-home pay.

Antenatal and postnatal care

A female employee is entitled to paid leave for antenatal and postnatal (up to 14 weeks following the birth) medical care.

The employee must give the organisation two week's written notice of any appointment and must be able to produce a certificate / record that the visit took place. Where possible, the appointments should be scheduled at the beginning or at the end of the working day. If the appointment finishes during the working day, she should return to work if this is practical.

A female employee is entitled to limited paid leave for antenatal classes. This leave is granted to expectant mothers and also to fathers, subject to:

- An expectant mother is entitled to paid time off to attend one set of antenatal classes, except for the last three classes in a set, for which unpaid leave or annual leave may be provided if they occur during normal working hours.
- A first-time expectant father is entitled to paid time off to attend the last two antenatal classes in a set of classes that the expectant mother is attending.
- An employee must give the organisation two weeks' notice in writing of the times and location of the classes. This written notification should be accompanied by an appointment card from the body running the classes.

Postponement of leave in the event of the child's hospitalisation

If the child falls ill and is hospitalised, and an employee has availed of at least 14 weeks' maternity leave with not less than four of those weeks being after the week of the birth, then she may apply to have the remaining maternity leave, and up to 16 weeks' additional maternity leave, postponed until the child is released from hospital. The decision to offer this postponement lies entirely at the discretion of the organisation.

An employee should request this postponement in writing to HR or her line manager as soon as possible, along with a letter confirming the hospitalisation of the child. The organisation should respond to requests as soon as is reasonably practicable after receipt.

Where the postponement is granted, an employee should return to work on an agreed date. The maximum period of postponement of leave is six months.

An employee must provide a letter or appropriate document from the hospital or the child's GP confirming the date that the child was discharged from hospital, before resuming maternity leave. Resumed leave must commence within seven days of the child's discharge from hospital.

If a female employee should fall ill during a period of postponement, and subsequently is absent from work, she will be deemed to have resumed maternity leave from the first day of absence. If the employee prefers to avail of sick leave, this must be done in line with the organisation's policies and procedures. It should be noted that, if an employee opts to transfer to sick leave, she forfeits her rights to any remaining maternity leave entitlements.

Should the female employee fall ill during additional maternity leave, or indicates that she intends to avail of additional maternity leave and then falls ill, she may apply to commence sick leave instead of taking the remaining additional maternity leave.

Death of the mother
In the unfortunate circumstances of the death of the mother within 40 weeks following the birth of a child, the father has a legal entitlement to remaining maternity leave during the 24 weeks following the death, with any additional leave being granted at the organisation's discretion.

Clearly, every effort should be made to accommodate the father during this time.

See also
Q11 What should be included in a remuneration package?
Q43 How many days annual leave are employees entitled to?
Q44 What public holidays are employees entitled to?
Q48 What are female employees' entitlements on their return to work after maternity leave?

Q48 What are female employees' entitlements on their return to work after maternity leave?

When maternity leave ends, a female employee is entitled to return to her usual job in so far as it is reasonably practical. However, if this is not possible, she should be offered suitable alternative work.

She must provide the organisation with at least four weeks' notice of her intention to return to work and her planned date of return.

She maintains all of her employee rights (other than remuneration) during maternity leave, including a full entitlement to annual leave and public holidays.

Postnatal care

A female employee is entitled to paid leave for postnatal medical care for up to 14 weeks following the birth, if this period falls outside her maternity leave.

She must give the organisation two week's written notice of any appointment and must be able to produce a certificate / record that the visit took place. Where possible, the appointments should be scheduled at the beginning or at the end of the working day. If the appointment finishes during the working day, she should return to work if this is practical.

Breastfeeding arrangements

For the purposes of the maternity legislation, 'breastfeeding' means breastfeeding a child or expressing breast milk and feeding it to a child immediately or storing it for the purposes of feeding it to a child at a later time.

If your employee is breastfeeding, then she is entitled to reduce her hours by one hour per day for the purposes of breastfeeding, for up to 26 weeks after the date of birth of the child, with no reduction in pay. Alternatively, she is entitled to work breaks equivalent to one hour per day for the purposes of breastfeeding in the workplace, for up to 26 weeks after the date of birth. Breastfeeding breaks may be taken as one 60-minute break, two 30-minute breaks, or three 20-minute breaks per day as agreed with the organisation.

Part time employees are entitled to a *pro rata* benefit to that provided to full-time employees.

See also
Q43   How many days annual leave are employees entitled to?
Q44   What public holidays are employees entitled to?
Q47   What are female employees' entitlements to maternity leave?

Q49 What are male employees' entitlements to paternity leave?

Paternity leave is not a statutory leave in Ireland, although many organisations offer paternity leave to their male employees on the birth of their child.

Such paternity leave is commonly between one and five days and is usually paid time off.

See also
Q11   What should be included in a remuneration package?

Q50   Can both parents take parental leave?

Yes, both parents can take parental leave. Each parent has their own entitlement to parental leave. In fact, every employee is entitled to take parental leave, whether they are the natural or adoptive parents, or what is called *in loco parentis* (Latin for 'in place of a parent').

Parental leave is statutory unpaid leave, the duration of which is 14 weeks.

The leave must be taken before the child reaches eight years of age, except in certain circumstances (for example, in the case of an adopted child, where there are some exceptions relating to the age of the child when adopted). In the case of a child with a disability, the age is 16 years.

Leave may be taken:

- As a continuous block of 14 weeks.
- Two separate blocks of not less than six weeks, with a minimum of 10 weeks between each block.
- By agreement with the employer, broken up over a period of time into individual weeks, days or hours.[4]

The employer can decide to postpone parental leave for up to six months. Generally only one such postponement is allowed, unless the reason for the postponement is based on seasonal variations in the volume of work, when the leave may be postponed for not more than two periods of six months in respect of the same child.

Finally, where an employee qualifies for parental leave in respect of more than one child, the employee may not take any more than 14 weeks' leave in any 12-month period, unless an employer agrees otherwise. However, this restriction does not apply in the case of multiple births (twins, triplets, etc).

---

[4]   Source: IBEC (2009). *Human Resources Management Guide*, Dublin: IBEC.

Note that even though this leave is unpaid, employees' statutory and contractual rights (with the exception of remuneration) are protected under the *Parental Leave Acts, 1998-2006*.

See also
Q11   What should be included in a remuneration package?
Q43   How many days annual leave are employees entitled to?
Q44   What public holidays are employees entitled to?

Q51   What are employees' entitlements to adoptive leave?

Employees in Ireland are entitled to adoptive leave under the *Adoptive Leave Acts, 1995-2005,* which provide a statutory right to leave for adopting female (and, in some situations, male, where he is the sole adopter) employees.

Adopting mothers (and, fathers, as above) are entitled to 24 weeks' leave, and a further 16 weeks' unpaid leave. An employee must apply in writing four weeks before their intended of taking this leave.

Other key points to note include:

- **Before:** Before an employee takes adoptive leave, they are entitled to time off to attend any preparation meetings or pre-adoption sessions.
- **During:** All employees' rights (except remuneration / pension) are protected during adoptive leave.
- **After:** Returning to work is treated the same as for an employee on maternity leave.

See also
Q11   What should be included in a remuneration package?
Q43   How many days annual leave are employees entitled to?
Q44   What public holidays are employees entitled to?

Q52 What are employees' entitlements to carers' leave?

Carer's leave is a statutory unpaid leave.

The entitlement to carer's leave applies to employees who have been employed for a continuous period of 12 months by an organisation.

If an employee is eligible, they may be entitled to leave from employment, to provide care for a person requiring it, for a period not exceeding 104 weeks, the duration of which must be agreed with the organisation. The organisation reserves the right to refuse applications for periods of carer's leave that are for less than 13 weeks, but must give such applications due consideration.

The person who the employee is proposing to provide full-time care and attention for must be deemed a 'relevant person' by a Deciding Officer from the Department of Social Protection, whose decision will be based on specific medical information relating to the person. A written decision from the Deciding Officer must accompany the completed Notice of Carer's Leave form. The organisation may request evidence from the employee that they are providing care and attention for the relevant person.

An employee is not entitled to carer's leave where another employee of the organisation is absent from employment, during the same period, on carer's leave for the same relevant person.

The period of carer's leave is unpaid and employees are limited in respect of any paid employment they may undertake during the period of carer's leave. The organisation should consider favourably requests from individuals on carer's leave for limited part-time working as permitted by the Department or as permitted under the *Carer's Leave Act, 2001*.

Employees may be entitled to Carer's Benefit (administered by the Department of Social Protection) but this entitlement is not a condition for entitlement to carer's leave from the employing organisation.

An employee must provide a minimum of six weeks' notice on a Notice of Carer's Leave form of their intention to commence carer's leave. In exceptional or emergency circumstances, this notice period may be waived and the organisation may accept notice as soon as is reasonably practicable.

In addition, not less than two weeks prior to the intended commencement date, a Carer's Leave Confirmation document must be signed and completed by both the employee and the organisation. A copy of the Deciding Officer's decision must accompany this document.

While an employee is on carer's leave, all statutory and contractual employment rights are protected – except the right to remuneration and superannuation benefits / contributions. The employee's right to annual leave and public holidays is maintained only during the first 13 weeks from the commencement date of the period of carer's leave. An employee's absence from work during a period of carer's leave is not treated as part of any other leave to which they may be entitled, such as sick, annual, adoptive, maternity, and parental or *force majeure* leave.

Usually, abuse of the entitlement to carer's leave results in termination of the leave and the commencement of disciplinary procedures.

Employees on carer's leave must notify the organisation in writing, not less than four weeks before the date on which they are due to return to work of their intention to return to work. They will return to their normal job on completion of the period of carer's leave insofar as is reasonably practicable or, if not, suitable alternative employment must be provided by the organisation.

See also
Q11   What should be included in a remuneration package?
Q43   How many days annual leave are employees entitled to?
Q44   What public holidays are employees entitled to?

Q53 Who is entitled to sick pay – and for how long?

There is no statutory obligation on most employers to provide an occupational sick pay scheme for employees. However, where an employee's contract provides a reference to sick pay entitlement, as part of the terms of employment, then a right to sick pay exists under contract law.

In an organisation where there is no formal sick pay scheme, but it is the norm for staff to be paid when absent through illness or injury, a right to paid sick pay may be established through custom and practice.

Some employments are covered by Registered Employment Agreements (REAs) with the Labour Court, which provide for sick pay benefits that employers are legally bound to pay. This situation may be affected by an announcement by the Minister for Jobs, Enterprise and Innovation of 'reforms to the Joint Labour Committee and Registered Employment Agreement wage settling mechanisms'.[5]

Currently, employees covered by a Joint Labour Committee (JLC) are entitled to sick pay benefits paid by their employer.

See also
Q11 What should be included in a remuneration package?

---

[5] See **www.djei.ie/press/2011/20110728a.htm**.

Q54   What compassionate leave should we allow employees?

Compassionate leave is not a statutory leave in Ireland.

Compassionate leave or bereavement leave is given at the discretion of an organisation, in situations where there may be a family crisis or death. Normally, non-statutory leave is unpaid but, due to the nature of this leave, most organisations continue to pay the employee as normal.

It is good practice to set out clear timelines for compassionate leave, depending on the circumstances – death of a spouse or child warranting longer leave than of a distant relative or non-relative.

See also
Q11   What should be included in a remuneration package?

Q55 How should we address dignity and diversity at work?

Dignity and diversity at work are intrinsically linked, and have become very topical in recent years, mainly due to the changing Irish workforce and demographics.

Diversity is a pro-active approach to employing a workforce where differences are embraced. Employing a diverse workforce can bring many advantages to an organisation, such as:

- A workforce representative of society at large (older, culturally aware, gender, race, religion, etc)
- An understanding of other cultures for the staff at large.
- A bigger recruitment pool.
- A competitive advantage for employers where staff understand the culture and nuances of a new market.
- Promoting the organisation's employer brand as an organisation where differences are embraced.

Equality legislation in Ireland specifically covers the following nine grounds on which discrimination is prohibited (and thus diversity is promoted):

- **Gender:** Man, woman or transsexual person (specific protection is provided for pregnant employees / maternity leave).
- **Marital status:** Single, married, separated, divorced or widowed.
- **Family status:** Parent of a person under 18 years or the primary carer or parent of a person with a disability.
- **Sexual orientation:** Gay, lesbian, bisexual or heterosexual.
- **Religion:** Different religious belief, background or outlook or none.
- **Age:** All ages above the maximum age at which a person is statutorily obliged to attend school (16 years of age).

- **Disability:** Broadly defined to include people with physical, intellectual, learning, cognitive or emotional disabilities and a range of medical conditions.
- **Race:** Face, skin colour, nationality or ethnic origin.
- **Membership of the Travelling community:** People who are commonly referred to as 'Travellers', who have a shared history, culture and traditions in a nomadic way of life in Ireland.

Addressing diversity

If your organisation wants to address or manage diversity, it requires a top-down approach, with support and buy-in from the senior management team.

Your organisation then should decide:

- What is the purpose of managing diversity?
- How will it achieve this?

Then your organisation must:

- Review the 'as is' situation in terms of diversity and draw up a 'proposed' outline for managing diversity, including targets.
- Review all recruitment processes, procedures and documentation to assess whether they cater for attracting a diverse workforce – for example, is the language clear and do advertisements adhere to equality guidelines.
- Develop a diversity policy to deliver an integrated approach to diversity across the organisation, which might include;
  - Accommodation of all religious views or dress codes.
  - Facilitating leave for employees who have to travel long distances.
  - Reviewing work night outs to cater for those who, perhaps for religious or other reasons, may find certain situations awkward.

See also
Q29   How do we protect ourselves from claims of bias or discrimination from unsuccessful candidates?

Q80 What do we do if an employee claims he / she is being bullied or harassed?

QUICK WIN LEADERSHIP, Q66 How should I manage diversity effectively?

Q56   How do we meet our obligations as an employer under the Working Time Act?

The *Organisation of Working Time Act, 1997* sets out statutory rights for employees in respect of rest, maximum working time and holidays. Organisations must ensure that they keep the following records to show compliance with the legislation:

- A copy of the written statement of terms of employment (contract).
- Details of all annual leave taken.
- Details of all public holidays taken.
- The name and address of each employee (including PPS no).
- Details of each employee's job and duties (job description).
- Details of days and total hours worked by each employee.
- Any other additional leave dates that were paid for.
- Any other details in respect of notice given to an employee.
- A record of rest breaks taken by each employee, unless the organisation uses some form of time and attendance system to manage these details (clocking in and out, for example) or notifies the staff member in writing of their breaks and, where the employee cannot take the break(s), they notify the employer of their inability to take the break(s).

An employer must hold all such records for at least three years after the employee has left their employment.

This is an area that confuses both organisations and employees equally. The advice above is necessarily basic and generic; for detailed advice specific to your organisation, check with your HR manager or legal advisor.

See also
Q35   What type of employment contract should we offer?

Q36   What must we include in an employment contract?
Q43   How many days annual leave are employees entitled to?
Q44   What public holidays are employees entitled to?
Q65   How do we support work-life balance for employees?

Q57 What responsibilities do we have, as an employer, for health and safety?

As an employer, your responsibility 'in so far as is reasonably practical' is to provide a safe and healthy place of work for your employees.

The Health & Safety Authority has outlined the key responsibilities of all concerned with health and safety in the workplace:[6]

- Managing and conducting all work activities so as to ensure the safety, health and welfare of people at work (including the prevention of improper conduct or behaviour likely to put employees at risk, including 'horseplay' and bullying).

- Designing, providing and maintaining a safe place of work that has safe access and egress, and uses plant and equipment that is safe and without risk to health.

- Prevention of risks from the use of any article or substance, or from exposure to physical agents, noise, vibration and ionising or other radiations.

- Planning, organising, performing, maintaining and, where appropriate, revising systems of work that are safe and without risk to health.

- Providing and maintaining welfare facilities for employees at the workplace.

- Providing information, instruction, training and supervision regarding safety and health to employees, in a form, manner, and language that they are likely to understand.

- Cooperating with other employers who share the workplace to ensure that safety and health measures apply to all employees

---

[6] HSA (2005). *A Short Guide to The Safety, Health and Welfare at Work Act, 2005*, Dublin: Health & Safety Authority, available at **www.hsa.ie/eng/ Publications_and_Forms/Publications/Safety_and_Health_Management/ Short_Guide to SHWWA_2005.pdf.**

(including fixed-term and temporary workers) and providing employees with all relevant safety and health information.

- Providing appropriate protective equipment and clothing to employees (at no cost to the employees).
- Appointing one or more competent persons to specifically advise the employer on compliance with the safety and health laws.
- Preventing risks to other people at the place of work.
- Ensuring that reportable accidents and dangerous occurrences are reported to the Health & Safety Authority.

All organisations also are required to carry out a risk assessment for the workplace to identify any hazards present, assess any risks arising from such hazards and identify the steps to be taken to deal with those risks.

An organisation also must prepare a safety statement based on the risk assessment. The statement should contain the details of employees who are responsible for safety matters. Employees should be given access to this statement and organisations should review it on a regular basis.

See also
Q58   What responsibilities do employees have for health and safety?
Q59   What should we do to provide a healthy and safe environment for employees?

QUICK WIN SAFETY MANAGEMENT

Q58   What responsibilities do employees have for health and safety?

Your organisation should ensure that not only does it comply with health and safety legislation, but also that your employees understand their responsibilities to:[7]

- Comply with relevant laws and protect their own safety and health, as well as the safety and health of anyone who may be affected by their acts or omissions at work.

- Ensure that they are not under the influence of any intoxicant to the extent that they could be a danger to themselves or others while at work.

- Cooperate with their employer with regard to safety, health and welfare at work.

- Not engage in any improper conduct that could endanger their safety or health or that of anyone else.

- Participate in safety and health training offered by their employer.

- Make proper use of all machinery, tools, substances, etc. and of all personal protective equipment provided for use at work.

- Report any defects in the place of work, equipment, etc. that might endanger safety and health.

Employees also should be made aware that, if they fail to observe and comply with the organisation's policies and procedures on health and safety matters, and as a result of their acts or omissions others are exposed to injury or risk of injury, they may be subject to the organisation's disciplinary procedure.

---

[7]   HSA (2005). *A Short Guide to The Safety, Health and Welfare at Work Act, 2005*, Dublin: Health & Safety Authority, available at **www.hsa.ie/eng/ Publications_and_Forms/Publications/Safety_and_Health_Management/ Short_Guide to SHWWA_2005.pdf.**

See also

Q57 What responsibilities do we have, as an employer, for health and safety?

Q59 What should we do to provide a healthy and safe environment for employees?

QUICK WIN SAFETY MANAGEMENT

Q59   What should we do to provide a healthy and safe environment for employees?

As an employer, an organisation must take all measures 'in so far as is reasonably practical' to ensure employees' safety, health and welfare at work (*Safety, Health and Welfare at Work Act, 2005*).

This means that:

- The safety system must be preventative.
- The workplace must be safe.
- The management is responsible for managing safety.
- Employers and employees must co-operate.

Therefore an employer must:

- Draw up a safety statement based on:
  - Identification of hazards.
  - Assessment of risks.
  - A statement of the preventative / control measures.
- Be aware of management's responsibility – safety must be an integral part of what management does on daily basis.
- Appoint a competent person to provide protective and preventative services.

See also
Q57 What responsibilities do we have, as an employer, for health and safety?
Q58 What responsibilities do employees have for health and safety?

QUICK WIN SAFETY MANAGEMENT

Q60 What is performance appraisal?

Performance appraisal is the process of assessing an employee's performance in order to ascertain their relevant strengths and weaknesses.

The success of performance appraisal systems largely depends on how well they are implemented, and how well they are integrated into an overall process of managing all employees' performance, their current and future roles, and their objectives to the overall organisational objectives.

Performance appraisal involves:

- Setting and agreeing goals between the employee and his / her line manager.
- Coaching.
- Recording information about the employee's performance.
- Making an appraisal of the employee's performance against the agreed goals.
- Discussing this appraisal with the employee at an appraisal review.
- Identifying gaps in performance.
- Addressing these gaps through a personal development plan.

Performance appraisal, when implemented properly, is an effective and fair way of managing performance, both from a management and an employee's perspective.

See also
Q41   What records do we need to hold on our employees?
Q61   When and how should we introduce performance appraisal?
Q62   How should we conduct a performance review with an employee?
Q63   How do we progress promotions fairly?
Q64   How do we deal with underperformance by an employee?

Q61 When and how should we introduce performance appraisal?

Performance appraisal should be an integral part of the performance management framework. It should be linked to the overall business objectives, so that individuals are clear in terms of their role and objectives in meeting the overall organisational goals.

The timing of the introduction of such a framework should be aligned with the overall business review cycle, so that they are inherently connected, and not seen as just another HR form to fill in!

Ask yourself the following questions. If the answer to any of them is "No", it may be time to introduce performance appraisal in your organisation:

- Are your employees' individual objectives and targets aligned to the overall organisational goals?
- Is the current system valued as part of the organisation's performance management system?
- Is the current system linked to pay?
- Is the current system linked to talent and succession planning?

The steps involved in introducing performance appraisal include:

- **Why performance appraisal?** Performance management aligns individual objectives to your overall organisational goals, and encourages a performance culture that ultimately underpins the achievement of your business targets. Performance management also assists in talent and succession planning for your organisation.
- **Have we senior management buy-in and support?** For the performance management framework to be successful, senior management buy-in and support is key.
- **Setting goals and objectives with the business:** While often the design of the performance management system is HR's responsibility, goal-setting must done by the line managers with their own staff (possibly supported by HR). Goals should be

SMART: specific, measurable, achievable, relevant and time bound.

- **Deciding on the performance review cycle:** Reviewing an employee's performance should be ongoing. That said, a formal review cycle is useful so that employees are prepared and understand where their performance is at during the course of the year – once a year reviews often result in an employee being shocked at the feedback. A good cycle combines informal one-to-one discussions on a monthly basis with mid- and end-year formal reviews.

- **Continuous review:** There should be a built-in mechanism for reviewing the system based on feedback from both employees and line managers.

See also

Q60 What is performance appraisal?
Q62 How should we conduct a performance review with an employee?
Q63 How do we progress promotions fairly?
Q64 How do we deal with underperformance by an employee?

Q62　How should we conduct a performance review with an employee?

Ideally, there should be a number of formal reviews of an employee's work performance throughout the course of the review cycle, in addition to ongoing informal discussions. These formal reviews should be documented and signed off by both the line manager and the employee.

At a formal performance review meeting, line managers should:

- Spend time in preparation for the meeting, seeking feedback from other managers / peers whom the employee works with (the employee should be made aware of this).
- Give honest, constructive feedback.
- Give examples of work well done and identify areas for development.
- Listen to what the employee has to say.
- Offer support.

At a formal performance review meeting, employees should:

- Be prepared for the meeting and bring any relevant feedback from other managers / peers or accolades, etc.
- Be able to accept constructive criticism.
- Feel comfortable that what is being reviewed is what they discussed and agreed with the line manager in earlier informal discussions.

Performance reviews should be a positive experience unless there is an underperformance issue or challenge.

When a performance appraisal process is linked to pay and reward, this is often agreed at the end of the year review.

See also
Q11　What should be included in a remuneration package?

Q12 How do we establish a fair remuneration package for a specific job?
Q60 What is performance appraisal?
Q61 When and how should we introduce performance appraisal?
Q63 How do we progress promotions fairly?
Q64 How do we deal with underperformance by an employee?

QUICK WIN LEADERSHIP, Q60 How can I make my performance appraisals produce better results for me?

Q63   How do we progress promotions fairly?

Ideally, all promotions should be advertised internally in an organisation, so that all employees have an opportunity to apply for the role, before looking externally to recruit.

The *Employment Equality Acts, 1998-2008* outlaw discrimination by employers with regard to access to employment, conditions of employment, training, promotion and classification of posts. The Acts describe discrimination as the treatment of a person in a less favourable way than another is, has been or would be treated in a comparable situation. Discrimination is outlawed on nine distinct grounds: gender, marital status, family status, sexual orientation, religion, age, disability, race and membership of the travelling community.

When considering the process your organisation uses for promotions, in the first instance you should ensure you avoid these nine grounds for discrimination.

Some organisations set out specific criteria for promotions to ensure both compliance with the law and fairness, equity and transparency in the promotion process.

See also
Q16   What are the best ways to recruit?
Q29   How do we protect ourselves from claims of bias or discrimination from unsuccessful candidates?
Q55   How should we address dignity and diversity at work?
Q60   What is performance appraisal?
Q61   When and how should we introduce performance appraisal?
Q62   How should we conduct a performance review with an employee?
Q64   How do we deal with underperformance by an employee?

Q64 How do we deal with underperformance by an employee?

It is the line manager's responsibility to manage both underperformance as well as good performance.

In the same way that the performance review is carried out, there are a number of steps to take in managing underperformance:

- Identify and agree the issue with the employee.
- Understand the reasons why there may be an issue.
- Agree an action plan with clearly defined timelines.
- Monitor the plan and follow up.

Only resort to disciplinary action in respect of underperformance when the approach above has been exhausted.

See also
Q60 What is performance appraisal?
Q61 When and how should we introduce performance appraisal?
Q62 How should we conduct a performance review with an employee?
Q63 How do we progress promotions fairly?
Q66 What should be included in our grievance and disciplinary policies?
Q68 What should be included in our disciplinary procedure?
Q70 How should our grievance and disciplinary policies be implemented?

QUICK WIN LEADERSHIP, Q54 How should I deal with difficult individuals in the team?

Q65 How do we support work-life balance for employees?

Most people strive to achieve an acceptable work-life balance for themselves. Work-life balance is not addressed specifically in Irish legislation, although the following pieces of legislation are relevant when trying to offer some flexibility to employees:

- *Protection of Employees (Part-time Work) Act, 2001.*
- *Employment Equality Acts, 1998-2008.*
- *Organisation of Working Time Act, 1997.*
- *Adoptive Leave Acts, 1995 & 2005.*
- *Carer's Leave Act, 2001.*
- *Parental Leave Acts, 1998 & 2006.*

Other work-life balance options for employees and employers include:

- Part-time working.
- Job-sharing.
- Job-splitting.
- Personalised hours.
- Compressed working week.
- Annualised hours.
- Term-time working.
- Time off in lieu.
- Flexi-time.
- E-working.
- Flexible leave arrangements.

In addition, there needs to be a culture within your organisation, led by senior management, that recognises the importance of work-life balance.

See also

Q56 How do we meet our obligations as an employer under the Working Time Act?

Q75 How do we respond to a request from an employee to work from home occasionally?

Q76 How do we manage employees who work from home regularly?

Q66   What should be included in our grievance and disciplinary policies?

Good grievance and disciplinary policies and procedures are key aspects of human resources management for your organisation. The underlying promise in all instances should be that:

- Everyone will be treated fairly.
- Any sanctions that may be imposed are clearly outlined.
- There is opportunity for recourse internally.

The *Code of Practice* drafted by the Labour Relations Commission (LRC) contains general guidelines on the application of grievance and disciplinary procedures and the promotion of best practice in giving effect to such procedures.

Grievance

A grievance policy allows employees to raise grievances with their employer. There are many reasons for an employee to have a grievance – the more common ones are:

- Pay.
- Dispute over performance ratings not conducted at a formal end-of-year performance review.
- Alleged bullying or harassment.
- Changing work practices.

Grievances should be dealt with immediately, as they often fester and result in a more much serious outcome than was potentially the case at the start. In any event, any grievance has the potential to be very serious and should be treated as such.

Disciplinary

A disciplinary policy sets out the basis for disciplining an employee and the disciplinary procedures set out the steps that will be followed by the organisation when serious or persistent breaches of the organisation's policies and procedures occur.

A copy of the disciplinary procedure should be given to a new employee within 28 days of starting work.

See also
Q67   What should be included in our grievance procedure?
Q68   What should be included in our disciplinary procedure?
Q69   What should be included in our disciplinary appeals procedure?
Q70   How should our grievance and disciplinary policies be implemented?

QUICK WIN LEADERSHIP, Q55 How should I handle employee grievances?
QUICK WIN LEADERSHIP, Q56 How should I discipline team-members?

Q67   What should be included in our grievance procedure?

It is always better to deal with any grievance informally at first. A cup of coffee to discuss an issue may be all it takes to resolve an employee's complaint. If not, and the employee wishes to take matters further, the formal stages of the grievance procedure then can come into play.

A best practice grievance procedure includes these stages:

- **Informal discussion:** An employee should be encouraged to approach their immediate line manager in the first instance to discuss issues and attempt to resolve them informally. If the employee is unsatisfied with the response, she / he may use Stage 1 of the procedure.

- **Stage 1:** The employee should be encouraged to approach a senior member of management and to notify them that they are invoking the first stage of the grievance procedure. A meeting should be held as soon as practical thereafter, at which the employee has the option of having a representative present at the meeting (a colleague of their choice or a trade union official). The issue should be discussed and a decision given to the employee within an agreed period of time. A summary of the meeting should be issued to those in attendance.

- **Stage 2:** If the employee is dissatisfied with the response given at Stage 1, they should approach the Managing Director / CEO or some other nominated person. The appeal may be verbal or in writing. A meeting should be held as soon as practical thereafter, at which the employee has the option of having a representative present at the meeting (a colleague of their choice or a trade union official). The issue should be discussed and a decision given to the employee within an agreed period of time. A summary of the meeting should be issued to those in attendance.

- **Stage 3:** If the response from Stage 2 does not resolve the issue, the employee should appeal to an appointed person / body. A meeting should be held as soon as practical thereafter, at which the employee has the option of having a representative present at the meeting (a colleague of their choice or a trade union official). The issue should be discussed and a decision given to the employee within an agreed period of time. A summary of the meeting should be issued to those in attendance. The decision of the appointed person / body now should be binding on all parties.

- **Further recourse:** If the employee feels that the response following Stage 3 is inadequate, they then may refer their grievance to the appropriate external body – for example, the Labour Relations Commission.

See also
Q66 What should be included in our grievance and disciplinary policies?
Q71 Is using a mediator the best option in grievance or disciplinary cases?

Q68   What should be included in our disciplinary procedure?

The disciplinary procedure is a core element of the overall employment relationship, and details should be issued to an employee within the first 28 days of being employed by your organisation.

Key points of a disciplinary procedure include:

- No disciplinary action should be taken against an employee until the matter has been appropriately investigated and a hearing conducted.

- At every stage of the procedure, the employee should be advised of the nature of the complaint against them and given an opportunity to state their case before any final or binding decision is made.

- The organisation should reserve the right at any stage of the procedure to suspend (with pay) an employee subject to the disciplinary procedure, in order for a full investigation into a complaint against the employee if the matter is serious or if such suspension is necessary for the investigation to take place.

- The employee should have the right to be accompanied by a work colleague or trade union official during the investigation or at any meeting connected with the investigation.

- The employee should have the right of appeal against any finding made against them.

- The employee should be informed of the outcome of the investigation as soon as practicable after its completion.

- The investigation should be carried out confidentially and in accordance with the law and the principles of natural justice.

Disciplinary procedure

The following disciplinary procedure is typical of that used by many organisations:

- **Verbal warning:** The employee should be advised of the reason for the warning and that it is the first stage of the organisation's disciplinary procedure. They also should be advised of their right of appeal as set out in your organisation's appeals procedure. A record of the verbal warning should be kept on the employee's personnel file but will be disregarded for disciplinary purposes after a defined period (usually six months) subject to satisfactory attendance, work performance or conduct in the meantime.

- **First written warning:** When an employee is issued with a first written warning, the details of the complaint, along with the improvement required and the timescale for improvement, should be given to them in writing. They should be warned that further action as set out will be considered if there is repetition of the conduct or where there is no satisfactory improvement. They should be advised of their right of appeal as set out in your organisation's appeals procedure. A copy of this first written warning should be kept on the employee's personnel file but will be disregarded for disciplinary purposes after a defined period (usually six months) subject to satisfactory attendance, work performance or conduct in the meantime.

- **Final written warning:** In the case of further repetition of earlier offences during a current warning period, or if the employee still fails to improve, or if the offence (whilst falling short of a breach justifying immediate dismissal) is serious enough to warrant only one written warning, the employee should be given a final written warning. This warning should set out the precise nature of the offence or complaint and contain a statement that a recurrence will lead to dismissal or whatever other penalty is considered appropriate and specifying, if appropriate, the improvement required and over what period. The warning should be placed on the employee's personnel file and will remain current for a period, usually 12 months. The employee should be advised of their right of appeal in relation to a final written warning as set out in your organisation's appeals procedure.

- **Dismissal:** In the case of gross misconduct, or if all previous levels of the procedure have been exhausted, the employee should be dismissed – but only after consideration of other possible disciplinary actions including (but without limitation) demotion, loss of seniority or pay or suspension with pay.

- **Summary dismissal:** The organisation should outline in its disciplinary policy its entitlement to dismiss an employee without notice in the event of gross misconduct or some other serious breach of the organisation's rules or of the terms and conditions of employment.

See also

Q41   What records do we need to hold on our employees?
Q66   What should be included in our grievance and disciplinary policies?
Q69   What should be included in our disciplinary appeals procedure?
Q70   How should our grievance and disciplinary policies be implemented?
Q71   Is using a mediator the best option in grievance or disciplinary cases?
Q83   On what grounds can we terminate an employee's contract?

Q69   What should be included in our disciplinary appeals procedure?

An employee always should have the right to appeal against the findings of your organisation's disciplinary procedure.

Typically, an appeals procedure operates as follows:

- If an employee wishes to appeal against any finding under the disciplinary procedure, they must deliver a letter of appeal to the organisation addressed to the nominated senior person of the organisation within five working days from the date they received notification of the decision, following the completion of the disciplinary investigation, stating that they wish to appeal such decision and the grounds of such appeal.

- The nominated senior person may nominate a member of management or other independent party to deal with the appeal in his / her place.

- The sanction imposed by the disciplinary process should be suspended until the outcome of the appeal process, but the employee may be suspended on full pay during the appeal process if the organisation believes that this is necessary in the circumstances.

- The employee should have the right to be accompanied at the hearing of their appeal by a work colleague or trade union official. Should the circumstances require it, the appeal hearing may be carried out by way of a full rehearing of the investigation.

See also

Q66   What should be included in our grievance and disciplinary policies?
Q68   What should be included in our disciplinary procedure?
Q70   How should our grievance and disciplinary policies be implemented?

Q70   How should our grievance and disciplinary policies be implemented?

Irish law states that an employer must issue an employee with a written statement of the disciplinary procedure, within 28 days of entering a contract of employment. There is no legal imperative to do so for the grievance procedure, although best practice suggests that an employee should be issued with the grievance procedure in the same timeframe.

The essential elements of a grievance and disciplinary policy, as outlined in the *Code of Practice, Grievance and Disciplinary Procedures* drafted by the Labour Relations Commission (LRC), are that:

- The procedures are rational and fair.
- The procedures are clear in terms of any disciplinary action.
- Any sanctions imposed are well defined.
- An internal appeal mechanism is available.

In the interest of good industrial relations, grievance and disciplinary procedures should be in writing and presented in a format and language that is easily understood.

Grievance and disciplinary procedures should be:

- Issued to all employees at the commencement of employment (or within 28 days thereof, as required by law).
- Included in induction training.
- Issued to trade unions representing employees.
- Issued to all managers / team leaders and others with responsibility for managing staff.

Best practice also requires a continuous review to ensure that adequate records are kept by the organisation.

All managers of staff, and all employees and their representatives, should be familiar with, and adhere to, the terms of the organisation's grievance and disciplinary procedures.

See also

Q6 What should be included in an employee handbook?
Q7 How do we communicate our employee handbook and its contents to employees?
Q39 Do we need an induction programme?
Q40 What should we include in an induction programme?
Q66 What should be included in our grievance and disciplinary policies?
Q67 What should be included in our grievance procedure?
Q68 What should be included in our disciplinary procedure?
Q69 What should be included in our disciplinary appeals procedure?

Q71 Is using a mediator the best option in grievance or disciplinary cases?

The Labour Relations Commission (LRC) defines workplace mediation as "a voluntary, confidential process that allows two or more disputing parties to resolve their conflict in a mutually agreeable way with the help of a neutral third party, a mediator".

Mediation gives staff involved in an issue an opportunity to address the issue and to explore options with an objective mediator, hopefully reaching an outcome that is acceptable to everyone through a mutually agreeable course of action.

Examples of issues that may arise in the workplace and benefit from mediation include:

- Breakdown in working relationships.
- Employee relation issues.
- Workplace interpersonal issues.
- Grievance issues (before they become disciplinary issues).

Workplace mediation is a flexible service that can be adapted depending on the situation. In essence, it allows each staff member an opportunity to give their side of the story, and ultimately to work with all other staff involved to find an agreeable solution. In practical terms, it may involve joint meetings and / or meetings alone with the mediator.

Importantly, workplace mediation is:

- **Voluntary:** Mediation can only take place when everyone agrees to take part in the mediation. Staff can withdraw at any stage if they are not comfortable.
- **Confidential:** Workplace mediation is completely private and confidential (unless the staff involved agree otherwise) in order to give staff the confidence to speak openly about the issue.
- **Fast:** Mediation can take place almost immediately an issue is raised.

- **Focused on reaching a solution:** Mediation focuses on reaching a solution for everyone.
- **Impartial and objective:** The mediator does not take sides but looks only to reach a satisfactory conclusion for all concerned.

There are many benefits to workplace mediation, including:

- Potential resolution of the issue and the outcome for action still lies with the staff members involved.
- Confidentiality at all times allows staff to have their voice heard.
- Its non-adversarial nature, which together with the confidentiality of the process, means that there is minimal risk for all involved.
- Even when a settlement cannot be achieved, the staff involved not only define the facts and issues of the dispute, but also have a mirror put up to their own views, thus assisting in preparing the ground for possible arbitration or court proceedings (should they proceed) in a more realistic light.
- Mediation, when staff are truly engaged, can have a longer lasting outcome than other outcomes.
- Other forms of dispute resolution are not affected by mediation.

The role of the mediator is crucial to the success of workplace mediation, so much so that an effective outcome is largely influenced by the quality and experience of the mediator. Thus, when seeking a mediator, talk to someone who has engaged a mediator previously and ask for a referral.

Finally, mediation can avoid often potentially very difficult disciplinary issues, and bring staff together to provide their own solution to a challenging situation.

See also
Q70 How should our grievance and disciplinary policies be implemented?

Q72   Can we prevent employees from joining a trade union?

Organisations cannot prevent employees from joining a trade union. Employees have the legal right to:

- Join a union – under Irish law, dismissing an employee for being a member of a trade union is deemed to be unfair.
- Join a union of their own choice.
- To leave a union.

However, there is no legal obligation on an organisation to recognise the employee's chosen union.

In practice, organisations often do recognise unions and draw up formal agreements covering a range of issues that affect their employees. Such an agreement might include (not exhaustive):

- The rationale for the agreement or a statement of the company's objectives regarding industrial relations.
- Date and time of the agreement and whether it is a fixed term agreement.
- Who is covered by the agreement.
- Where and how disputes or issues may be resolved – the process.
- Representatives – who represents the union from among the organisation's employees and how they are selected.
- Meetings.
- Grievance / disputes procedures.
- Working arrangements.
- Disciplinary procedures.

Many organisations promote positive employee relations and offer staff representation instead of, or sometimes as well as, recognising a union. Staff associations can represent staff in the same way that a union might. Like unions, they usually work within an agreement drawn up between the organisation and the staff association covering a broad range of issues affecting employees.

See also

Q73 Are employees entitled to paid time off during working hours to attend to union duties?

Q73　Are employees entitled to paid time off during working hours to attend to union duties?

The Labour Relations Commission (LRC) sets out guidelines in its *Code of Practice*, relating specifically to the duties and responsibilities of employee representatives. In general, employee representatives should be afforded reasonable time off to attend to their union duties. If there is no formal agreement in place outlining these times, then reasonable limits may be set.

Employee representatives who carry out their duties and responsibilities should not:

- Be treated unfairly, including changes or amendments to their pay and conditions as a result of their role, or be selected unfairly for redundancy.
- Be dismissed for carrying out their duties.

Depending on the size and complexity of the organisation, and the level of activity that the employee representative is involved in, it should be agreed beforehand whether an employee should be paid in respect of all time spent on their union duties.

See also
Q72　Can we prevent employees from joining a trade union?

Q74 How can interns / work placements help us cope with sudden changes in staffing needs?

Interns, cooperative education programmes or undergraduate placement schemes can be a source of support during times of labour shortage or sudden increases in workload.

Many companies offer internships to students, usually for a period of between six and nine months. Some courses at universities offer students the option of securing a work placement for one year (generally before their final year) before they enter their final year; in other universities, the placement is a core element of the course.

Undergraduate placement programmes provide organisations with:

- An opportunity to undertake specific projects or other work by hiring students without adding a permanent payroll cost.
- A cost-effective solution to a (short-term) recruitment gap.
- Students who are generally very eager to learn.
- A chance to vet potential graduates first-hand over an extended period in a real work environment, thus developing a recruitment pipeline.
- A straightforward process for recruiting graduates.

From a student's perspective, the work placement / internship:

- Gives hands-on experience while completing their studies.
- Builds self-confidence by working with others.
- Puts theory into practice.
- Broadens their knowledge base.
- Increases the student's chance of securing a role with that organisation.
- Helps to develop skills such as team working, decision-making, communication and numeracy.

- Helps them to understand different cultures, if working overseas.
- Provides real-life experience of the work environment and how it operates.
- Informs decisions about their future career.

See also

Q2   How do we establish our staffing needs?
Q3   How do we decide between doing work in-house and outsourcing it?
Q33   What do we do if we cannot identify suitable candidates in Ireland and want to recruit from outside Ireland?
Q34   How do we manage a recruitment freeze?
Q96   We are restructuring our business – where do we start?

Q75   How do we respond to a request from an employee to work from home occasionally?

Not all jobs or employees are suited to home-working – for example, roles that require a lot of face-to-face conversations clearly do not lend themselves to working from home.

However, roles with clearly defined objectives and outcomes that are easily measurable and that require minimum supervision lend themselves to home-working more easily.

When an employee asks whether they can work from home occasionally, it is not enough simply to agree in order to accommodate the individual – working from home must work for the organisation also.

It is a worthwhile exercise to revisit the original job description and understand what may have changed to warrant now working from home. Also other staff may be disappointed that their own role was not selected for home-working, so the rationale to allow a specific instance of home-working must be robust, fair and transparent.

In terms of the person, there are particular characteristics and personality types that tend to work from home more successfully than others. Typically, these people:

- Are self-motivated.
- Do not require much social interaction.
- Have very well-developed time management skills.

As with all new initiatives, it is worth considering running a pilot project initially, to see whether it works and to iron out any issues that may arise before implementing home-working across the wider organisation.

See also
Q65   How do we support work-life balance for employees?
Q76   How do we manage employees who work from home regularly?

Q76 How do we manage employees who work from home regularly?

Working from home, e-working, or peripatetic working (working in different places) are all part of the changes in the way employees work now. The *Safety, Health and Welfare at Work Act, 2005* obliges organisations to ensure the health and safety of their employees, including those who are not based onsite.

For employers, the alleged loss of management is a big factor in managing staff who work from home regularly. For this type of arrangement to work, it is important that:

- There are very clearly defined objectives and targets for the employee to achieve.
- There is a strong element of trust between the employee and their line manager.
- The employee only works some days from home, and so does not become too isolated from other employees in the office.
- There are regular set calls with the office-based team members for updates.
- The person working from home attends some, if not all, of the team's meetings.
- The employer is aware of its responsibilities regarding a home office, including the responsibility to furnish and prepare it.

Working from home regularly can be very rewarding, particularly if employees are working on projects that require quietness and time to think.

As with all new initiatives, it is worth considering running a pilot project initially, to see whether it works and to iron out any issues that may arise before implementing home-working across the wider organisation.

See also

Q57 What responsibilities do we have, as an employer, for health and safety?

Q58 What responsibilities do employees have for health and safety?

Q59 What should we do to provide a healthy and safe environment for employees?

Q65 How do we support work-life balance for employees?

Q75 How do we respond to a request from an employee to work from home occasionally?

Q77   How should we deal with absenteeism?

Strictly, 'absence' includes both certified and uncertified medical leave and approved absence, whether paid or unpaid. However, in HR terms, 'absence' generally is used to refer to unapproved absences, often without prior notice, from the workplace.

Every organisation should have an absence policy and a fair procedure for dealing with it, which might include:

- A clear explanation as to why absence is unacceptable – the pattern, the duration, the days. It is important the employee fully understands why their absence is unacceptable.

- Discussion with the employee (return-to-work consultation), listening to what they have to say with regard to absence on their return to work. At this point, the organisation may refer the employee to the company doctor for a second opinion in cases of claimed illness or, in some cases, may invoke disciplinary procedures.

- A process to identify the real reason (which may not be the reason stated) for absence from work. Perhaps there are personal or work issues, where the organisation can support the employee and help them make progress, thus ensuring that they are not absent in the future.

- A clear understanding of the outcomes, up to and including dismissal for those who do not improve.

- Occupational advice in some instances.

- Preventative measures – including flexible working arrangements, reviewing the recruitment process and the induction programme.

The maintenance of absence records is crucial in providing evidence on actual absenteeism and its costs, patterns and trends. When this information is available, your organisation can review the data and agree reasonable reduced targets for absenteeism in order to reduce costs and gain a full understanding of the scale of the problem.

It is usually the line manager's responsibility to:

- Conduct the return-to-work meeting with the employee.
- Retain all records related to absence.
- Liaise with HR where appropriate.
- Liaise with the company doctor where appropriate.

An absence policy is a key aspect of managing absence as it sets out clearly what is expected of employees so there should be no surprises when they are asked to meet with their line manager on their return from absence!

See also
Q41   What records do we need to hold on our employees?
Q64   How do we deal with underperformance by an employee?
Q65   How do we support work-life balance for employees?

Q78   How do we conduct an investigation into alleged wrongdoing at work by an employee?

If a situation of alleged wrongdoing at work arises where it has been decided that an investigation should take place, there are a number of stages that should be followed to ensure that the investigation is carried out correctly.

If there is an obvious breach or an issue is very clear-cut, then it may be possible to hold the investigation and the disciplinary interview at the same time.

Typically, the investigation process proceeds as follows:[8]

- Inform in writing all employees included in the investigation that an investigation is taking place and furnish them with all relevant information. This letter should include the nature of the issue, the date and venue of the investigation meeting, details of the organisation's disciplinary procedure. It also should communicate the employee's right to representation.

- Depending on the seriousness of the situation, the organisation may decide to suspend an employee with pay at this point, pending the outcome of the investigation (this option should be included in the letter also).

- The employee should confirm whether they can attend the investigation meeting, and who will be their representative.

- If the employee comes to the meeting without a representative, remind them of their right to representation – if they decide not to bring a representative, this may go against the employer at a later hearing should there be one.

---

[8]   IBEC (2009). *Human Resources Management Guide*, Dublin: IBEC.

- Appoint an independent investigator – anyone who has been involved in the disciplinary process at any point should be excluded from any further role in the investigation.

- The investigation meeting usually involves the investigator, the employee and their representative. Depending on the nature of the investigation, it may be necessary to invite witnesses to corroborate evidence given by the employee – although this usually happens at a later date. During the interview, put all evidence, questions and any other relevant information to the employee, who should be asked to respond. Outline all sanctions to the employee and explain that no decision will be made until all the evidence has been heard, and that the issue then may be referred to a disciplinary meeting.

- At the end of the meeting, summarise the interview in writing – everyone present at the meeting should sign this summary.

- The investigator then should issue a report with his / her recommendation either for clearance of the employee of any wrongdoing or for disciplinary action against the employee.

- The next stage is the disciplinary meeting, prior to which the employee should be provided with the investigator's report and asked to attend the meeting with their representative. At this meeting, the employee should present their case to the disciplinary authority (the manager hearing the case), who will listen and decide on what sanction(s) should be taken.

- In the event that the employee is not satisfied with the outcome of the disciplinary procedure, he / she then has the right to use the organisation's appeal procedure.

See also

Q66 What should be included in our grievance and disciplinary policies?
Q68 What should be included in our disciplinary procedure?
Q69 What should be included in our disciplinary appeals procedure?
Q70 How should our grievance and disciplinary policies be implemented?

Q79 Should we have a data protection policy?

Every organisation should have a data protection policy. The *Data Protection Acts 1988-2003* set out the rules and principles that companies must follow and adhere to when processing, maintaining and storing personal data about individuals, both employees and customers. They also give individuals (employees, as well as customers) certain rights in relation to personal data that is held about them, in electronic form (on your organisation's computer system) and manually (in documents on the employee's personal file).

Organisations must ensure that all personal information is:

- Obtained and processed fairly.
- Used and disclosed only for specified, explicit and legitimate purposes.
- Adequate, relevant and not excessive.
- Accurate, up-to-date and complete.
- Retained only for as long as required to complete the purpose specified for such information.
- Kept safe and secure.
- Not further processed in a manner incompatible with the purposes for which it was obtained.
- Not transferred outside the European Economic Area without adequate levels of data protection.

Personal data is data relating to a living individual who is or can be identified either from the data or from the data in conjunction with other information that is in, or is likely to come into, the possession of the organisation. Examples of personal data held in the records of an organisation include an employee's address, age, contact details, bank details and position, etc. CCTV images are also a form of personal data. Note that, in some cases, line managers may hold employee information in their own files, outside the organisation's formal systems.

'Sensitive personal data' is personal data relating to a person's racial or ethnic origin, political opinions, religious or philosophical beliefs, trade union membership, physical or mental health, sexual life, criminal convictions or the alleged commission of an offence, and proceedings for an offence committed or alleged to have been committed. For example, most organisations collect and process sensitive personal data in respect of their employees' health or trade union membership, where necessary in connection with the individual's employment.

'Processing' includes the obtaining, recording, keeping or disclosing of data. Processing of employee personal data may be done only with the consent of the person to whom it relates. However, such consent is not required where, for example, the processing is necessary for compliance with a legal obligation or is necessary for the performance of a contract to which the employee is a party (participation in an employee benefit scheme). When processing sensitive personal data, the organisation has additional obligations.

To ensure compliance with the law, it is important that:

- An organisation has a data protection policy in place.
- All employees read, understand and implement the data protection policy.

See also

Q41   What records do we need to hold on our employees?

QUICK WIN MEDIA LAW IRELAND, Q77 What are the fundamentals of data protection legislation?

QUICK WIN MEDIA LAW IRELAND, Q78 How is data protection law enforced?

Q80   What do we do if an employee claims he / she is being bullied or harassed?

Bullying and harassment are complex areas to deal with, because they depend on a person's perception of what it is to be bullied or harassed: what may be fun for one person may be bullying for another.

Bullying and harassment is outlawed in Ireland, and any breach should be dealt in line with your organisation's disciplinary procedures. Employees should be made aware that serious and / or persistent breaches of the policy will be treated by the organisation as gross misconduct and may result in dismissal.

The *Report of the Taskforce on Workplace Bullying* (March 2001) defined bullying as "repeated inappropriate behaviour, direct or indirect, whether verbal, physical or otherwise, conducted by one or more persons against another or others, at the place of work and / or in the course of employment, which could reasonably be regarded as undermining the individual's right to dignity at work".

Examples of bullying behaviour include verbal abuse, threats, jokes, isolation or exclusion from social activities, pestering people, imposition of impossible deadlines, giving one individual all the unpleasant work and so forth.

Harassment is any form of unwanted conduct related to any of the following grounds: gender, marital status, family status, sexual orientation, religion, age, disability, race or membership of the travelling community ground. It can be perpetrated by management, colleagues, subordinates, clients or other business contacts. Harassment in any form is unacceptable and is a form of discrimination that can affect the confidence, morale, performance and health of the person being harassed and therefore is a very serious issue.

Victimisation occurs where a person is treated less favourably than another because he / she in good faith has made a complaint to his / her employer in relation to harassment or bullying behaviour or has sought to exercise any of his / her rights under the *Employment Equality Acts, 1998-2004*.

In the event that an employee believes that he / she is being or has been harassed, bullied or victimised by a fellow employee, client or business contact, they should report the matter to their line manager as soon as possible. In the event that the harassment, bullying or victimisation is caused or condoned by the line manager, then the employee should report the matter to a senior manager or the CEO / MD of the organisation.

It is important that all incidents of harassment, bullying or victimisation are reported, as the organisation cannot take action unless and until such incidents are reported.

All complaints of harassment, bullying or victimisation should be dealt with sensitively and as quickly and confidentially as possible.

See also

Q78 How do we conduct an investigation into alleged wrongdoing at work by an employee?

Q81   What should be included in an email policy?

Due to the permanent nature of e-mails and the potential legal implications to both the organisation and its employees, the following should be included in an email policy:

- Email messages should be written and formatted in the same manner as standard written communications from the organisation.

- The wording, tone and language should be appropriate, concise and carefully prepared in order to avoid ambiguity, inaccuracy, defamatory remarks, breach of confidentiality and the possibility of offence. Use of mobile phone 'text speak', such as 'u' instead of 'you' is not acceptable.

- Emails relating to business transactions and containing matters of client information must be printed out and be retained in hard copy on the client's file.

- All external communications with clients, associates and suppliers must be considered for the relevance of content, accuracy, and potential to commit the organisation to business transactions or exposure to legal liability. Therefore, such communications should be carefully considered before being sent and, in case of doubt, a line manager consulted.

- Appropriate disclaimers should be put on all e-mails, letters, reports, and any other relevant documentation.

- Files or attachments received *via* electronic communications from third parties (clients, associates, suppliers etc) may be copyright protected. Therefore, care should be taken in forwarding or distributing any information contained in the files or attachments to avoid breach of such copyright, and, in case of doubt, a line manager consulted.

- Data contained in emails may be subject to the provisions of the data protection or freedom of information legislation.

- Forging or attempting to forge an email or disguising or attempting to disguise an email when sending should be strictly prohibited.

- Before leaving the office for a day off or vacation, employees should activate an 'out of office' autoresponse to emails, advising the length of their absence / date of their return and to whom queries should be addressed in their absence.

An email policy should reinforce the organisation's position that discriminatory comment, aggression, harassment or bullying or comments based on age, gender, race, religion, disability, marital status, family status, sexual orientation or membership of the travelling community is not acceptable in internal or external emails. Any person found sending this type of email should be subject to the organisation's disciplinary procedures, up to and including immediate dismissal.

It is best that the policy in my view is detailed and does not allow for any ambiguity.

See also
Q66 What should be included in our grievance and disciplinary policies?
Q68 What should be included in our disciplinary procedure?
Q69 What should be included in our disciplinary appeals procedure?
Q70 How should our grievance and disciplinary policies be implemented?

QUICK WIN MEDIA LAW IRELAND, Q37 Can emails be defamatory?

Q82   What pension rights do employees have?

When it comes to pensions, employees have many rights: statutory, organisational and individual.

Many people in Ireland are entitled to a State pension (also known as the 'old age pension'), of which there are two main types:

- **Contributory:** To which people over 66 years of age, who have worked and paid social insurance, are entitled.

- **Non-contributory:** A means-tested pension available to those who do not qualify for a contributory State pension.

Changes were made to State pensions in 2011, particularly around the definition of retirement age. For more information, see: **www.citizensinformation.ie/en/social_welfare/social_welfare_paymen ts/older_and_retired_people/**.

From an organisation's perspective, there is no statutory obligation on employers to offer a pension scheme to employees. Employees are entitled to a pension scheme only if it is included in their employment contract.

Some employments provide for a pension scheme through a Registered Employment Agreement (REA) or Employment Regulation Order (ERO), both of which are agreements registered by the Labour Relations Commission. Where this is the case, the employer and employees are legally bound by the agreement and the rules of the scheme. This situation may be affected by an announcement by the Minister for Jobs, Enterprise and Innovation of 'reforms to the Joint Labour Committee and Registered Employment Agreement wage settling mechanisms'.[9]

If there is no pension scheme on offer, the organisation must offer access to a Personal Retirement Savings Account (PRSA), introduced by the *Pensions Amendment Act, 2002*. A PRSA is essentially an individual's own personal transportable pension scheme. The obligation on the employer

---

[9]   See **www.djei.ie/press/2011/20110728a.htm**.

is merely to offer access to the scheme and to facilitate the employee's contributions to it – there is no requirement on an employer to contribute to an employee's PRSA. If an organisation offers a PRSA, the necessary information should be provided in writing to employees.

See also
Q12   How do we establish a fair remuneration package for a specific job?

AFTER
EMPLOYMENT

Q83 On what grounds can we terminate an employee's contract?

The most common reason for terminating an employee's contract is because they have done something wrong. When this happens, an investigation takes place and sanctions are imposed as a result, one of which may be dismissal.

If an organisation wishes to terminate an employee's contract for any other reason, it must have very strong reasons for doing do so – otherwise, unfair dismissal legislation will protect the employee.

For example, if an employer wishes to terminate an employee's contract because the employee:

- Is not doing his / her job properly, the organisation should ensure that it has followed proper procedure in line with performance management before doing so.
- Does not have the required qualifications anymore (most of the cases that are heard on this relate to the loss of a driving licence). From an employer's perspective, it is important that all relevant documentation (contract, disciplinary procedure, handbook, etc) states that, if an employee cannot work because they do not have the relevant qualifications and they have not tried to upskill, they can be redeployed and / or dismissed. Before dismissing an employee in this situation, the organisation must offer support for retraining.
- Has not performed satisfactorily during their probationary period, the organisation must ensure it is doing so appropriately and that the employee has had sufficient, documented feedback throughout the course of their probation, and has no basis to take a claim against the employer for unfair dismissal.

See also
Q38 What is probation –and how does it work?
Q64 How do we deal with underperformance by an employee?

Q66 What should be included in our grievance and disciplinary policies?

Q68 What should be included in our disciplinary procedure?

Q69 What should be included in our disciplinary appeals procedure?

Q70 How should our grievance and disciplinary policies be implemented?

Q78 How do we conduct an investigation into alleged wrongdoing at work by an employee?

Q84 When is it legal to terminate without a notice period?

Q84 When is it legal to terminate without a notice period?

The only instance where it is in order to terminate an employee's contract with an organisation without notice is where the employer dismisses an employee because of the employee's gross misconduct.

Gross misconduct is usually understood to be something very serious – theft, gross negligence or something similar – that warrants summary dismissal without any notice.

In all other situations, dismissal of an employee without notice runs the risk of a claim for unfair dismissal.

However, where an employee resigns or claims redundancy as a result of lay-off or short-time working, they are not entitled to a notice period or payment for a notice period, since they terminated the employment not the employer.

See also
Q66 What should be included in our grievance and disciplinary policies?
Q68 What should be included in our disciplinary procedure?
Q69 What should be included in our disciplinary appeals procedure?
Q70 How should our grievance and disciplinary policies be implemented?

Q85 What is constructive dismissal?

Constructive dismissal occurs when an employee feels that, because of the actions of their employer, they have no option but to resign. Unlike in unfair dismissal cases, the onus of proof in constructive dismissal lies with the employee.

An employee will win their claim of constructive dismissal under the *Unfair Dismissals Acts, 1997-2007* only if they can prove that their resignation was warranted by the actions of their employer. If an employee is found to have been unfairly dismissed, they may be placed back in their job, or more commonly, they may receive compensation for the loss of earnings caused by the dismissal.

A contract is terminated for the purposes of constructive dismissal:

- When the employer is in actual breach of the employment contract.
- When the employer does not wish to be bound by one or more essential terms of the contract.
- When the employer has acted unreasonably – the onus of proof is on the employee to prove that the employer has acted so.

Employees are expected to have acted reasonably themselves before pursuing a claim for constructive dismissal, in that they are expected to:

- Prove their resignation was warranted.
- Show that they pursued the organisation's grievance procedures in the first instance.
- Show that that they explored all industrial relations options (up to and including the Rights Commissioner) before resigning.
- Show that they only resigned as a last resort.

See also
Q36 What must we include in an employment contract?
Q66 What should be included in our grievance and disciplinary policies?
Q67 What should be included in our grievance procedure?

Q86   Should we conduct exit interviews with all leaving employees?

It is best practice to conduct exit interviews with leaving employees. Exit interviews can offer insights into the reasons why employees leave or move on to other organisations. Sometimes, these conversations appear to be fruitless, as ex-employees often do not want to say why they 'really' left – particularly, if they left because of an individual manager, or any other sensitive reason. Nonetheless, the information from exit interviews builds up over time, allowing trends to be assessed.

The aim is to obtain robust information both immediately and over time, to understand what your organisation can improve on in relation to:

- **Recruitment:** Are you recruiting the right people if they are leaving?
- **Remuneration:** Are you paying market rates?
- **Retention:** Is there something else you could do to retain staff?
- Management style.
- Training and development.

Over time, this information has real value and can inform policy-making – for example:

- If the main reason employees are leaving the organisation is because of pay, then there is an immediate action in terms of analysis for key 'flight risk' staff in the short-term, and longer term a full review of the remuneration policy.
- If one of the main reasons for leaving the organisation is because of lack of promotional opportunity, then an immediate action may be to look at all recent promotions and explore whether high-performing staff are being catered for in terms of their career. A longer term review of talent and succession also should be considered.

Policy-making decisions for the organisation will not be decided on exit interview data alone, but in tandem with other data it can be very powerful indeed.

Ideally, an exit interview should be face-to-face but increasingly organisations outsource exit interviews, and an external company calls the ex-employee after they have left the organisation. There are pros and cons to this, insofar as employees are more likely to say how they feel to someone who is not part of the organisation, although conversely a face-to-face meeting with their own manager may be more meaningful overall.

The best time for an employee to be honest is when they are leaving since they can be open in what they say without worrying what it might do to their career. Equally, if they are leaving on good terms, it offers them an opportunity to speak openly about minor niggles.

However, although exit interviews can be useful, there is no requirement on employees to take part and they can decline an invitation.

See also
Q87   How should we conduct an exit interview?
Q100   How do we steal a march on our competitors with a better
           recruitment experience for candidates?

QUICK WIN LEADERSHIP, Q68 Why are exit interviews important?

Q87   How should we conduct an exit interview?

An exit interview has a slightly different tone and feel to a traditional recruitment and selection interview. Typically, it involves set questions to which the employee gives a straight "Yes" or "No" answer.

It is still important to put the employee at ease, especially since you want the interview to be meaningful and to gain a full understanding as to why the individual is leaving.

When the employee is relaxed, you can start the exit interview by asking questions such as:

- Why have you decided to leave the organisation?
- Why did you choose the company you are going to?
- Is there anything we could have done to encourage you to stay?
- What did you enjoy most about your job?
- What did you enjoy least about your job?
- Do you feel you had the full support you needed to do your job to the best of your ability?
- Did you receive all the training and development you needed to do your job properly?
- Would you consider working with us again sometime in the future?
- What type of remuneration package are you leaving for?
- Is there anything you would like to add or comment on before we close?

It is important to wish the employee well and to end the interview on a positive note.

See also
Q86   Should we conduct exit interviews with all leaving employees?

Q88 Should we give references to leaving employees – and what should we say / not say?

It is up to you as an employer whether you want to give references to leaving employees, as there is no statutory obligation on you to do so.

Most employers want to give references, particularly where the relationship with the leaving employee was a good one. In addition, since they are likely to look for references themselves when recruiting, there is a moral obligation to provide other organisations with references for leaving employees.

Often, due to the size of an organisation and increasing litigation, references only refer to the role, tenure, etc and do not go into any detail on the employee's performance. Smaller companies tend to give more information in this regard.

As an employer, if you are issuing references to leaving employees, it is incumbent on you and your organisation to issue objective, fair references.

Also consider the following;

- Always ensure what you say is objective and not out of malice.
- Always act fairly and reasonably – stick to the facts.
- Where the reference is a questionnaire, only answer those questions where you have factual answers.
- If the reference depends on reports from internal sources, then always check carefully to ensure the accuracy of these sources, especially where you have no personal knowledge of the employee or their work.
- Never send a reference by email or fax for reasons of privacy or risk of a defamation claim.
- Where a reference is requested over the telephone, always check the details of the caller before responding.

If you are in the course of settling any employment litigation in respect of the employee for whom the reference has been requested, only give a reference on the basis of legal advice.

And, in all cases, if you are in any doubt when giving references, always take independent legal advice.

See also
Q31   Should a job offer be subject to a satisfactory reference check?

Q89   When is TUPE relevant?

Transfer of undertakings (protection of employment) (TUPE) legislation covers employees' contractual rights when a business is transferred. In the current climate of closures, takeovers, mergers, and restructures, redundancy and transfers are a regular occurrence.

The original 1980 legislation has been the subject of many court judgements at European level, as well as in UK and Irish jurisdictions. As a result, revisions by way of Regulation have brought about three main changes:

- A mandatory consultation period of 30 days with employees before the date of transfer.
- An employee can seek redress for alleged breaches of the Regulations during the transfer and up to six months afterwards.
- The criminal jurisdiction for alleged breaches under the previous instruments was repealed.

Importantly, the Regulations cover all employees, employers in undertakings, and all and part of businesses that are transferred to another employer as a result of the legal transfer or merger.

Much of the confusion relating to TUPE has to do with deciding when a transfer occurs. The European Court of Justice (ECJ) has deemed there to be a transfer when these three points all apply:

- There is a change in employer.
- The activity transfers as a going concern.
- The business retains its identity upon the transfer.

For example:

- A company contracts out part of its business.
- A state Department or agency transfers funding for services provided from one employer to another.

- A new lessee of premises continues a business the same as or similar to that previously carried out by the previous lessee (for example, a restaurant).

However, the area of outsourcing or contracting out has caused some of the greatest discussion and controversy. Contracting out is not specifically referred to in the Directive, or in the Regulations. That said, the ECJ has confirmed that, in many different situations, there has been a transfer where there has been a change in the provider of a service under a contract. Normally, this change has come about because:

- The company contracts out part of its business (for example, cleaning or catering).
- The company decides to change contractors (the business is already contracted out).

When it is deemed that a transfer has taken place, the rights and obligations of the original employer *vis-à-vis* the employee by way of contract of employment are transferred to the new employer. Continuity of employment is preserved, unless the employee has received redundancy from the original employer during the transfer. In this situation, if the employee continues to work for the new employer, they do so as if in a new role.

Where a transferred employee is dismissed by the new employer, the termination is based on the minimum notice contained in the employee's original contract of employment and / or the statutory notice based on length of (original continued) service. Both periods of employment are similarly considered under the Unfair Dismissals legislation.

The Regulations accommodate economic reasons for dismissal, but the reasons must be justified on the basis of 'economic, technical or organisational reasons entailing changes in the workforce'.

Whether employees have representatives or not, transferors and transferees are obliged to consult with the employees directly in writing or through their representatives or nominated representatives not less than 30 days before the transfer in relation to:

- The date or proposed date of the transfer.

- The reasons for the transfer.
- The legal implications of the transfer.
- Any measures envisaged in relations to the employees.

Failure to notify the employees can result in a right of action in any court for compensation.

The TUPE Regulations normally are enforced through the Employment Appeals Tribunal and the civil courts. Complaints regarding an alleged breach should be made to a Rights Commissioner within six months of the alleged contravention (12 months in exceptional circumstances).

Finally, the TUPE legislation is confusing and is constantly and regularly being tested in the courts, so legal advice is essential. The key message in all cases, however, is employees are entitled to terms and conditions no less favourable than they had with their previous employer.

See also
Q3   How do we decide between doing work in-house and outsourcing it?
Q92   When is redundancy applicable?
Q94   What steps do we need to take to make someone redundant fairly?
Q96   We are restructuring our business – where do we start?

Q90   Can we recover pay from a former employee?

The first point when looking to recover pay from an employee or former employee is to understand the specific reasons for the recovery – there are many conditions that may or may not apply as a result.

The *Payment of Wages Act, 1991* lays down very specific requirements for a valid deduction from wages or receipt of a payment from an employee. A deduction from, or payment by, the employee must:

- Be required or authorised by law.
- Be under a prior and still valid oral or written term of the contract.
- Have the employee's written consent.

A deduction is only legal if it relates to:

- Any act or omission of the employee (including suspension without pay, as well as fines for breakages, shortages, etc).
- Any goods or services supplied to or provided for the employee, the supply or provision of which is necessary to the employment.

Also, some conditions must be met:

- Before an incident that gives rise to a deduction, an employee must be given a copy of the written term of the contract or written notice of the existence of an oral term.
- Before the deduction is made, the employee must be given one week's prior written notice of the act of omission that gave rise to it and the amount to be deducted.
- The employer should not delay more than six months after discovering the act / omission before making the deduction.
- The deduction must be fair and reasonable in all circumstances – the employee should not be left with too little to live on in cases other than suspensions.

- A deduction in respect of loss or damage suffered by the employer, resulting from an act or omission by the employee, must not exceed the amount of loss or damage.

In addition, an employer may make deductions from wages or receive payments from employees in respect of:

- Recovery of overpayments of wages or expenses made (for any reason) by the employer to the employee, provided the amount of the deduction does not exceed the amount of the overpayment.

- A deduction made or payment received arising from disciplinary proceedings.

- A deduction made by the employer from the employee's wages under the following arrangements:
  - Under a term of a contract between the employer and the employee, the inclusion of which in the contract the employee has given prior written consent or to which the employee has otherwise given written consent.
  - Under which the employer deducts and pays to a third person amounts that the third person has given written notice of being due to him / her from the employee. Such deductions are valid if they are made in accordance with the notice and are paid not later than the date specified in the notice.
  - A deduction in respect of the employee's participation in a strike or other industrial action.
  - A deduction made or payment received in whole or partial satisfaction of an order of an employee to the employer or to a third party – for example, a maintenance order.

Finally, all the conditions to a particular deduction / payment must be met if it is to be valid, and a receipt must be given to an employee from whom an employer receives payment.

Q91   Must all employees serve out their notice period?

Legally, there is a requirement that minimum notice is given by both employers and employees prior to an employee leaving an organisation.

The period of notice legally due to employees varies according to their length of service with the company. These notice periods can be, and are often, increased by employers but can never be reduced below the legal minimum.

Length of Service	Minimum Notice [10]
13 weeks – 2 years	1 week
2 years – 5 years	2 weeks
5 years – 10 years	4 weeks
10 years – 15 years	6 weeks
More than 15 years	8 weeks

An employee does not always have to serve out his / her notice period – for example, when the employee is:

- **Paid in lieu of their notice:** In this instance, an employee or employer waives the right to notice. This is a mutual agreement, and the employee accepts payment in lieu of that notice. This payment is considered the same as a termination payment and can be treated from a tax perspective in the same way. The employee's termination date remains the same as if he / she worked out their notice period.

- **Offered 'gardening leave':** This occurs when an employee who has resigned or has been dismissed works out their notice at home and is paid until the notice period ends. This practice occurs mainly where there is sensitive information that the employer is concerned the employee may use after they leave (sales people

---

[10]   Source: IBEC (2009). *Human Resources Management Guide*, Dublin: IBEC.

with access to customer records, for example) or where the employee is being investigated and they are asked to stay at home.

- Summarily dismissed due to gross misconduct.

An employee who is willing and able to work during their notice period is entitled to normal pay whether or not work is available.

See also
Q84 When is it legal to terminate without a notice period?

Q92   When is redundancy applicable?

Organisations must be very clear when considering redundancy that it is the *role* which is made redundant, not a *person*. It follows then that the employee is dismissed when their role is no longer exists (by reason of redundancy). Redundancy should not be seen as an easy way to address a performance issue.

A role is considered to be redundant if, for example (not exhaustive):[11]

- An employer is no longer trading or ceases to carry out the business for the purpose of which the employee was employed.

- The organisation has to restructure and ultimately rationalise numbers, and the employee's role is 'at risk of redundancy'.

- The employee's work may be done by another person who also can perform other work which the employee is not qualified for, or the work can be done in a completely different way.

The needs of the business are a key decider in making a role redundant. The role should be longer required and, as a result (and only as a result), the employee may be dismissed by reason of redundancy.

See also
Q3   How do we decide between doing work in-house and outsourcing it?
Q89   When is TUPE relevant?
Q93   When does last in, first out apply in selecting employees for redundancies?
Q94   What steps do we need to take to make someone redundant fairly?
Q97   What is the difference between redundancy and voluntary severance?

---

[11]   Source: IBEC (2009). *Human Resources Management Guide*, Dublin: IBEC.

Q93 When does last in, first out apply in selecting employees for redundancies?

LIFO (last in first out) is a term that has long been associated with redundancy. However, with changing legislation regarding age, equality, etc, it should be used carefully.

The selection process for redundancy is one of the most important aspects of redundancy, in order to ensure fairness and transparency.

Selection for redundancy should be absolutely objective and based on set criteria that ensure no-one is treated unfairly. Discrimination is defined in the *Employment Equality Acts, 1998-2004* as "treating a person less favourably that another is, has been, or would be treated" – this applies for the purpose of redundancy also. Discrimination may occur where an employee is treated less favourably than another for one or more of any of the following reasons: gender, marital / family status, religion, disability, colour, sexual orientation, age, race, nationality / ethnic origin including membership of the travelling community.

So although LIFO is simple to implement in a redundancy situation, and at one level appears fair, it may not be. In essence, before your company decides to make a role redundant, plan it carefully, and consider all the relevant legislation.

See also
Q92 When is redundancy applicable?
Q94 What steps do we need to take to make someone redundant fairly?
Q97 What is the difference between redundancy and voluntary severance?

Q94   What steps do we need to take to make someone redundant fairly?

Here's some sound advice if you are considering implementing redundancy:

- Selection for redundancy needs to be fair and transparent – how you decide on particular individuals over others (person over the role, one role over another, age, length of service and skill set, etc.) is a deciding factor in whether the redundancy has been fair, if it becomes litigious at any later point.

- Ensure as an organisation that the redundancy message is delivered clearly and concisely (factual and practical).

- Employees must be given not less than two weeks' notice in writing (before the date of dismissal) of the proposed dismissal and may be entitled to longer notice under their contract of employment.

- A copy of the certificate of redundancy, form RP50, or other written notice of redundancy must be given to the employee at least two weeks before the date on which the redundancy is due to take effect (the fine for not giving adequate notice or false information is up to €5,000).

If you have to defend a redundancy decision against a claim for unfair dismissal, how you approached the redundancy – both the process and the rationale – is of the utmost importance.

See also

Q92   When is redundancy applicable?
Q93   When does last in, first out apply in selecting employees for redundancies?
Q97   What is the difference between redundancy and voluntary severance?

Q95 Do we need a confidentiality policy?

More and more, organisations are concerned with confidentiality. Competitive advantage in a downturn is more important than ever and, as a result, organisations are keen to protect themselves.

Employees often are asked sign confidentiality and non-disclosure agreements agreeing to keep confidential and secret, during and after their employment with the organisation, all information obtained during their employment with the organisation, whether disclosed by the organisation verbally or in writing or learnt by observation. Often these agreements are a condition of employment.

See also
Q36 What must we include in an employment contract?

Q96 We are restructuring our business – where do we start?

First, the decision to restructure is a strategic decision to be taken by the Board of Directors and the executive team (including, ideally, a HR Director) with input from other senior leaders in the organisation.

It is fundamental to any successful restructuring that HR is involved, both at a senior level in terms of strategic direction and at operational level(s) tactically for business design or restructure and implementation.

In a restructuring, the elements to consider before moving to the design phase include:

- What is the rationale for the restructure? Is cost a primary factor, or improved delivery, or a change of terms and conditions for staff, or a combination of all of the above?
- Is here a budget for the restructuring?
- Have timelines been set?
- Are there enough resources available to deliver what is required?

Then, in terms of moving to the design of the new structure and implementation, the key areas for focus are:

- The project governance and team.
- Clearly-defined objectives and milestones for the project.
- Regular project team meetings (weekly, if it is a big project).
- Staff assigned to the project for the duration.
- Workable chunks of work for each team member.

The restructure then moves through the different phases of the project to ensure delivery to the agreed timelines:

- **Phase 1:** Work with the line managers to see clearly the 'as is' and 'proposed' structures. Then highlight areas where there may be challenges – for example:
  - Who are the key stakeholders?

- Budget – financial and headcount?
- Will the current skill set transfer to the new structure?
- Will there be a redundancy situation (if so, this may affect the timelines)?
- Is the organisation unionised (if so, this may affect timelines)?
- Are there technical and infrastructural dependencies?

- **Phase 2:** When these issues have been worked through and the new structure agreed and signed off, the project moves into Phase 2, which focuses on the transition from the 'as is' to the proposed structure. Important points to consider here are:
  - Ongoing communications with all key stakeholders.
  - The process for transition including people and processes – for example, will there a competition for the new roles and what are the salary implications? Are there opt-out options?

- **Phase 3:** Phase 3 of the project is post-implementation and continuous review:
  - Is the new structure working well and delivering to agreed service level agreements (SLAs) or key performance indicators (KPIs)?
  - Has any there been any turnover during transition and implementation?
  - Are there opportunities to amend and review and fine tune?

These phases are not exhaustive in terms of activities or approach, but give a blueprint for the methodology / process that you should consider before embarking on any restructure, rationalisation or streamlining of your organisation.

See also

Q3   How do we decide between doing work in-house and outsourcing it?
Q89   When is TUPE relevant?
Q92   When is redundancy applicable?

Q97 What is the difference between redundancy and voluntary severance?

Redundancy and voluntary severance (VS – also known as voluntary redundancy (VR)) both mean essentially that a job / role is 'at risk of redundancy'. However, from an employee's point of view, there is a significant difference between the two, in that the 'voluntary' nature of VS/VR still leaves them with a measure of choice.

In a redundancy situation, the role is made redundant and the employee has no option but to leave, because there is no longer a job for them.

In a VS/VR situation, the role is made redundant and the employee is offered a choice of remaining employed by the organisation – in a different, usually less attractive role, although with the same terms and conditions – or of taking a severance package. If the organisation's aim is to reduce headcount often a VS/VR package will be more attractive than might be offered in a redundancy situation. The key is that the choice of remaining or leaving lies with the employee in a VS/VR situation.

See also
Q92 When is redundancy applicable?
Q93 When does last in, first out apply in selecting employees for redundancies?
Q94 What steps do we need to take to make someone redundant fairly?

HR MANAGEMENT

Q98 What is the responsibility of HR in a downturn?

Prior to this recession, the focus for HR typically was on supporting growth in our organisations. From an HR perspective, this meant activities such as attraction and selection, talent management, pay and reward and development were a priority. It also meant, more importantly, partnering with the business units to deliver a common goal for growth.

Priorities today see HR still partnering the business units but now to deliver cost reductions in the form of redundancies, pay cuts or freezes, and reductions in training and development, not to mention an increased employee relations (ER) agenda. This sometimes can leave HR isolated, now assisting in making redundant people who last year we were working with side-by-side to deliver on the growth agenda.

Closer to home, this recession sees HR departments themselves reduced substantially in headcount thereby leaving more work for remaining colleagues. All of this added work, often perceived as less fulfilling, leaves HR under pressure to deliver more, in a more challenging environment, with less resources and experience.

To alleviate this pressure, HR can / should:

- Stay focused.
- Agree and contract new priorities with line managers so everyone is clear what is to be delivered.
- Meet regularly with business contacts and update them on progress against plan.
- Explain that HR are impacted too.
- Enjoy! This is a great opportunity to gain experience in areas that may not have been available to you before now.

This is a time for HR to shine, to take a lead role at the senior management table, and to deliver to the business agenda as never before. Businesses will rely on HR more than ever during this recession, to deliver cost rationalisation plans and other such initiatives to ensure their survival. From an HR perspective, surely there can be no greater opportunity.

See also

Q96   We are restructuring our business – where do we start?

Q99   When do we need to employ an interim HR professional?

The role of the interim HR professional will survive and thrive during these times of recession.

HR roles are no more immune to redundancy than any other. In fact, in many large organisations, due to cost, the role of the HR director or senior HR manager may be made redundant or not replaced on retirement / departure. However, there is a real risk in this: losing senior people purely on a cost basis at a time when their skills and experience are most needed may leave your organisation at risk also.

This is where the interim HR professional can provide support, in both the delivery of value-added HR solutions for the business and any rationalisation or restructure and/ or potential employee relations issues. The advantage of such HR professionals is their ability to integrate quickly, with a wide range of skills, from wide-ranging experience in employee relations and reward to stakeholder management and project management.

The most successful interim HR professionals in this new environment will:

- Be flexible in terms of hours and pay.
- Be experienced in all areas of HR, with particular focus on employee / industrial relations.
- Have strong stakeholder / relationship management skills.
- Take responsibility for their decisions.
- Be willing to give their opinion.
- Research new client organisations – to understand their business and key priorities quickly.
- Roll up their sleeves and not mind what work they do.
- Offer pragmatic advice, particularly to small organisations where there are no internal support mechanisms.

- Be CIPD-qualified.

The interim professional can work with a company for an agreed specified time where there is a cost outlined upfront to the company and a clear understanding that, when the work is complete, the HR professional will leave.

See also
Q6 What should be included in an employee handbook?

Q100   How do we steal a march on our competitors with a better recruitment experience for candidates?

How organisations treat candidates, whether they are successful or unsuccessful, from application, through screening to selection or being declined, is known as the 'candidate experience' – and can vary in quality, to say the least!

In a recession, when there are fewer roles to fill, and the market is flooded with candidates, there may be little sense of urgency to reply to applicants – to all applicants. Nonetheless, organisations and their HR professionals have the perfect opportunity to steal a march on the competition by offering a positive candidate experience. If you treat applicants and candidates well and with dignity, they will speak well of your organisation as a result, to your longer-term benefit.

Recruitment is the first interaction for a potential employee (or customer – they may be a customer even if they never become an employee) with your organisation. Through social networking, your brand can be damaged instantly. The candidate experience you offer ultimately affects performance, employee engagement, retention and your (employer) brand. Can you afford not to make this investment – even in a recession?

See also
Q86   Should we conduct exit interviews with all leaving employees?
Q98   What is the responsibility of HR in a downturn?

BIBLIOGRAPHY

Armstrong, M. (1999). *Human Resource Management Practice*, 7th edition, London: Kogan Page.

Carr, A. (1999). *The Development of an Induction Programme for FEXCO*, published B.Sc.(HRM) thesis, DIT.

Citizens Information, Public Service Information website **www.citizensinformation.ie**.

Department of Jobs, Enterprise and Innovation website **www.djei.ie**.

HSA (2005). *A Short Guide to The Safety, Health and Welfare at Work Act, 2005*, Dublin: Health & Safety Authority, available at **www.hsa.ie/eng/Publications_and_Forms/Publications/Safety_and _Health_Management/Short_Guide to SHWWA_2005.pdf**.

IBEC (2009). *Human Resources Management Guide*, Dublin: IBEC.

Irish Statute Book website **www.irishstatutebook.ie**.

Labour Relations Commission (2000). *Code of Practice: Grievance and Disciplinary Procedures*, Dublin: Labour Relations Commission.

Labour Relations Commission, Ireland website **www.lrc.ie**

National Employment Rights Authority website **www.employmentrights.ie**.

Torrington, D., Hall, L. and Taylor, S. (2008). *Human Resource Management*, 7th edition, London: FT Prentice Hall.

University of Limerick Cooperative Education and Careers Division website **www.ul.ie/careers**.

ABOUT THE AUTHOR

ANGELA CARR is Principal at Carr McCrea & Associates which she founded in 2009. Carr McCrea (**www.carrmccrea.ie**) is a niche HR consulting firm, bringing a project management approach to HR. Angela has over 17 years' experience in senior HR roles, latterly as part of a senior HR management team, and Head of Resourcing for a large global financial institution.

Angela graduated 1st in Year with a BSc Management (HR) DIT, and was an international badminton player, representing Ireland numerous times at all levels.

A regular contributor to HR and business publications including *Accounting & Business*, *HR & Recruitment Ireland* and *BusinessPlus*, Angela was featured in *IMAGE* magazine's November 2010 edition as one of Ireland's Top Business Women.

ABOUT THE QUICK WIN SERIES

The **Quick Win** series of books, apps and websites is designed for the modern, busy reader, who wants to learn enough to complete the immediate task at hand, but needs to see the information in context.

Topics published to date include:

- QUICK WIN B2B SALES.
- QUICK WIN DIGITAL MARKETING.
- QUICK WIN ECONOMICS.
- QUICK WIN LEADERSHIP.
- QUICK WIN MARKETING.
- QUICK WIN MEDIA LAW IRELAND.
- QUICK WIN SAFETY MANAGEMENT.

Topics planned for 2011 include:

- QUICK WIN COMMUNICATION.
- QUICK WIN PRESENTATIONS.
- QUICK WIN SMALL BUSINESS.

For more information, see **www.oaktreepress.com**.

Lightning Source UK Ltd.
Milton Keynes UK
UKOW051433230911

179177UK00002B/1/P